New Perspectives on the Structure of Transnational Criminal Justice

Transnational Crime

Volumes published in this Brill Research Perspectives title are listed at *brill.com/rptc*

New Perspectives on the Structure of Transnational Criminal Justice

Edited by

Mikkel Jarle Christensen
Neil Boister

BRILL

LEIDEN | BOSTON

This paperback book edition is simultaneously published as issue 1.2–3 (2017) of *Transnational Crime*, DOI 10.1163/24680931-12340002.

Library of Congress Control Number: 2018930994

Typeface for the Latin, Greek, and Cyrillic scripts: "Brill". See and download: brill.com/brill-typeface.

ISBN 978-90-04-36578-0 (paperback)
ISBN 978-90-04-36579-7 (e-book)

This book is printed on acid-free paper and produced in a sustainable manner.

Contents

New Perspectives on the Structure of Transnational Criminal Justice

Mikkel Jarle Christensen and Neil Boister

Transnational Criminal Justice: Its Politics and Practices

The expansion of what is now commonly referred to as globalisation has increased and added to the variety of the goods, ideas and people moving across state borders. While globalisation itself is a contentious term that has been debated at least since the end of the Cold War,[1] it is safe to say that this social, political and economic transformation has contributed to the opening of new illegal as well as of new legal markets. The creation of globalised flows of money, goods and services, built upon new forms of technology and the proliferation of competitively priced mass transportation. Today, for example, the internet allows individual consumers to engage in cross-border commerce, legal and illegal, from the comfort of their home. While such transactions may begin in virtual space in which new forms of transnational cybercrime have evolved, their effects are also material. As a result of electronic commerce and communication, a wide array of products are transported across borders by large freight companies by air, sea and road. The low costs of such transport allow products consumed in the Global North to be produced cheaply in the Global South. This system of global capitalism hinges on almost 680 million annual container moves.[2] The material nature of globalisation has also affected crime patterns and the perception of crime. Just as legal production and commerce has increasingly used the gap between the developed and developing world to increase profit margins, new lucrative transnational markets for illegal products and services have been established as an undercurrent of globalisation, often taking advantage of the same technologies, modes of transportation and asymmetries between rich and poor to ensure a profitable balance between demand and supply. For the perception of crime, the globalisation of crime

1 Frank J. Lechner and John Boli, *The Globalization Reader* (5th edn, Wiley 2014) 1.

2 World Bank, 'Container port traffic' (2014) <http://data.worldbank.org/indicator/IS.SHP.GOOD.TU> accessed 13.11.2017.

 | DOI 10.1163/9789004365797_002

patterns has been linked especially to the growth of organized crime, and very often also to the changed migration patterns in the Global North, in effect morphing the image of the immigrant with that of the criminal.[3]

While cross-border or transnational crime is a long-standing practice that predates the current phase of globalisation,[4] this acceleration of movement and communication has not only offered new openings for criminals, it has also created new opportunities for the criminal justice systems that fight them. In parallel to a reconfiguration of the power balances between national security institutions, most notably the police and the military,[5] the perception of crime has shifted as security has been reimagined around crime rather than around defense. As part of this development, the globalisation of crime has garnered increased attention from governments, international organisations and academics.[6] In response to what is perceived to be an acceleration of new forms of transnational crime, national criminal justice systems have reorganised to face new crime patterns whether related to specific problems such as drugs trafficking and terrorism or to more general forms of organised crime operating across national borders. At regional and international levels, new legal tools have been created to harmonise national approaches to transnational crime and to create more favorable conditions for collaboration between national law enforcement units.[7] New perceptions of global crime were driven in part by national criminal justice systems that promoted their new transnational capabilities as a necessesary and important innovation and thus helped construct global crime as a societal problem in need of a solution that they could deliver.

In this larger space, the concept of transnational criminal law has come to describe the legal technologies constructed or reconfigured to provide the framework for criminalisation, harmonisation and cooperation targeting specific forms of criminal behavior. Theoretically, the concept of transnational

3 Didier Bigo, 'Globalized (in)security: The field and the ban-opticon' in Didier Bigo and Anastassia Tsoukala (eds), *Terror, Insecurity and Liberty: Illiberal practices of liberal regimes after 9/11* (Routledge 2008) 10.

4 Peter Andreas, *Smuggler Nation: How Illicit Trade Made America* (New York: OUP 2013) 2.

5 Didier Bigo, 'When two become one' in Morten Kelstrup and Michael Charles Williams (eds), *International relations theory and the politics of European integration: Power, security, and community* (Routledge 2000) 171.

6 David Nelken, 'The Globalization of Crime and Criminal Justice' (Oxford) 50 Current Legal Problems 251.

7 See generally Didier Bigo, *Mapping the Field of EU Internal Security Agencies* (L'Harmattan 2007); Ben Bowling and J.W.E Shetycki (eds), *Global policing* (Los Angeles, Calif.; London: SAGE 2012); J.W.E. Sheptycki (ed), *Issues in Transnational Policing* (Routledge 2000).

criminal law builds partly on perceptions of transnational crime as developed by legal scholars and criminologists[8] and partly on the concept of transnational law as developed by Phillip Jessup.[9] Neil Boister has contributed the most comprehensive account of the characteristics of transnational criminal law as a dualistic system of law that builds on international frameworks for cooperation between states, while still jealously guarding their sovereignty over criminal law.[10] This perspective differentiates transnational criminal law as a system that targets private crimes from the system of international criminal law that, at least in theory, has direct jurisdiction over crimes of public concern, the so-called core international crimes.[11] While precisely which crimes ought to be codified as international crimes has remained contentious[12] and has been the object of debate among criminal justice stakeholders themselves,[13] theoretically, at least, the distinction between the two is fairly clear. In practice, however, the overlap between the two spaces of criminal justice is less clear-cut as recent scholarship has shown.[14] Taking its cue from such overlaps, the present special issue investigates the political, legal and social dynamics that characterize the structure of transnational criminal justice as a practical endeavour.

8 Gerhard O.W. Mueller, 'Transnational crime: definitions and concepts' in Phil Williams and Dimitri Vlassis (eds), *Combatting Transnational Crime: Concepts, Activities and Responses* (London: Frank Cass 2001) 13; Roger Cotterrell, 'The Concept of Crime and Transnational Networks of Community' in Valsamis Mitsilegas, Peter Aldridge and Leonidas Cheliotis (eds), *Globalisation, Criminal Law and Criminal Justice: Theoretical, Comparative and Transnational Perspectives* (Hart 2014) 7.

9 Philip Jessup, *Transnational law* (Yale University Press 1956).

10 Neil Boister, 'Further reflections on the concept of transnational criminal law' [Routledge] Transnational Legal Theory (6)1; Neil Boister, *An Introduction to Transnational Criminal Law* (0199605386, Oxford University Press 2012); Neil Boister, 'Transnational Criminal Law?' 14 *European Journal of International Law* 953.

11 Andrew Clapham and Paola Gaeta, *War Crimes and Other International 'Core' Crimes* (Oxford University Press 2014).

12 Regina Menachery Paulose, 'Beyond the core: incorporating transnational crimes into the Rome statute' (2012) 21 *Cardozo Journal of International & Comparative Law* 77; Neil Boister, 'The Exclusion of Treaty Crimes from the Jurisdiction of the Proposed International Criminal Court: Law, Pragmatism, Politics' 3 J Armed Conflict L 27.

13 Mikkel Jarle Christensen, 'Crafting and Promoting International Crimes: A Controversy between Legal Professionals of Core Crimes and Anti-Corruption' 30 *Leiden Journal of International Law* 501.

14 Mikkel Jarle Christensen and Ron Levi, 'Introduction: An Internationalized Criminal Justice: Paths of Law and Paths of Police' in Mikke Jarle Christensen and Ron Levi (eds), *International Practices of Criminal Law: Social and Legal Perspectives* (Routledge forthcoming 2017).

With this collective aim, the papers try to push beyond the legal and theoretical distinction between international and transnational criminal law. They do so by changing the perspective from the *law* proper to the *justice* practices, technologies and agents that drive engagement with the law and, to some extent, construct its boundaries and reach. The main idea with this exercise is to further develop—and in some cases challenge—the legal conception of transnational criminal law by investigating what we call transnational criminal justice as a broader phenomenon. Critically testing and challenging this conception by bringing together social science and legal scholarship, we hope to strengthen the theoretical conceptualisation of this space of law and justice and provide it with a more empirical foundation. Collectively, the papers in this special issue investigate the main symbolic and material characteristics of this space of law, how it is organised and what social and political dynamics shape its functionality and impact.

1 Politics, Law and Social Dynamics

Although the individual papers take different theoretical standpoints and thus contribute distinct findings, the common question is how transnational criminal justice is structured as a space in which the law is shaped by politics and different social dynamics, such as those that play out between different types of professionals, and how these structures are best conceptualised. From this common point of departure, three different analytical dimensions run through the articles. One focuses on the political provenance of technologies and networks of transnational criminal law and how their genesis has shaped their development and function. Another zooms in on the legal frameworks crafted as a result of these political processes and investigates their form, content and effects on law enforcement strategies and practices. A final dimension takes one step further towards criminal justice practices by analysing the social constitution of transnational criminal law, its agents and how the power balance between them affects perceptions of crime and criminal justice in this wider space. These dimensions are not mutually exclusive, and while the individual articles often focus on one of them they each try to situate their analysis of transnational criminal justice in a larger social space.

In terms of politics, the space of transnational criminal law draws on a long incremental history of development that has its modern roots in bilateral relations built around the suppression of slave trading and the refinement of extradition of non-political fugitives in the nineteenth century. These initiatives slowly morphed into a broader multilateral treaty making process in the League of Nations era, slowly gathered momentum in the post-war period and then transformed into a boom of investments into new forms of law that occurred from the 1970s. Despite the East/West divide that characterised international politics during the Cold War, the legal diplomacy around transnational criminal law, organized under the broader banner of 'international criminal law'[15] became very active during this period. A number of what would now be considered, returning to Boister's terminology, crime suppression conventions were adopted and supported by States from East and West, including the 1961 Single Convention on Narcotic Drugs,[16] the 1973 Convention on the Prevention and Punishment of Crimes against Internationally Protected Persons including Diplomatic Agents,[17] and the 1979 International Convention against the Taking of Hostages.[18] Cold War diplomacy did not stifle all development of international criminal law instruments, but did affect the scope of cooperation and the intensity of enforcement mechanisms written into these conventions. From the 1990s, other legislative players have entered to arena including the highly influential Financial Action Task Force, which promulgates and monitors 'soft law' recommendations with a hard compliance edge,[19] and the Security Council, which directly legislates obligations on states to enact new domestic offences tackling aspects of transnational crime that it considers threaten international peace and security.[20] While still relying on the direct application of criminalisation through states, these interventions introduced a new, more directive dimension into transnational criminal law with provisions that were not as open to being watered down, for example, as those settled by states participating on an equal footing in the development of suppression conventions.

Perestroika transformed the foreign policy position of the Soviet Union and helped open up a new space for international institution-building in the 1990s in a period where China was also more open to such initiatives.[21] One effect of this period was the creation of the field of international criminal justice as

---

15 M. Cherif Bassiouni, *International Criminal Law* (Transnational Publishers 1986).

16 New York, 30 March 1961, 520 UNTS 151; in force 13 December 1964.

17 New York, 14 December 1973, 1035 UNTS 167, in force 20 February 1977.

18 New York, 17 December 1979, 1316 UNTS 205, in force 6 March 1983.

19 The FATF Recommendations: International Standards on Combating Money Laundering and the Financing of Terrorism and Proliferation, 16 February 2012, updated October 2016. See generally C. Rose, *International Anti-Corruption Norms: Their creation and Influence on Domestic Legal Systems* (Oxford: OUP, 2015), 2.

20 Cian Murphy, 'Transnational Counter-terrorism Law: Law, Power and Legitimacy in the 'Wars on Terror' (2015) 6(1) *Transnational Legal Theory* 31.

21 Karen J. Alter, *The New Terrain of International Law: Courts, Politics, Rights* (Princeton University Press 2014) 42.

a space targeting core international crimes.[22] The USSR and China both supported the building of the first international criminal court since Nuremberg, the International Criminal Tribunal for the former Yugoslavia (ICTY) and innovations in this field were supported by parallel currents of legal and political investments from, at different times, the US, Europe, Latin America and African countries. The result of this development was the creation of a social and legal space with its own particular dynamics.[23] This process of differentiation and specialization helped narrow the conception of international criminal law that is now seen as relating to core international crimes only. It was against this background that a new system of transnational criminal law was re-conceptualised, building on previous scholarship as something different by systematising and theorising the connection between the private crimes that were not deemed properly international. In contrast to international criminal justice, transnational criminal law rules and practices remained formally and operationally dominated by national states, although the states are supported by international institutions and organisations that also operate in this space, such as Interpol, the UN, the EU and the Council of Europe. However, despite the active participation of these institutions, the criminal justice system of national states, or what Max Weber would call their legitimate monopoly over the authority to exercise power,[24] remains at the core of transnational criminal law and is crucial for understanding the politics and legal diplomacy of this space.

The second dimension in the special issue deals specifically with the forms of law and regulation that have developed in this space. As an emerging scholarly sub-discipline, transnational criminal law is focused on systematizing the myriad of more than 200 multilateral and many thousand bilateral and national legal instruments that make up this form of law. Academic interest in this new area was partly based on an identified discrepancy in the attention legal scholars have given to international crimes[25] and that afforded to transnational crime.[26] By theoretically building the coherence transnational criminal law, legal scholars contributed original perspectives on the legal developments in this space as well as the differences and commonalities that characterise

22 John Hagan and Ron Levi, 'Crimes of War and the Force of Law' 83 Social Forces 1499.

23 Mikkel Jarle Christensen, 'From Symbolic Surge to Closing Courts: The Transformation of International Criminal Justice and its Professional Practices' 34 *International Journal of Law, Crime and Justice* 609.

24 Max Weber, 'Politics as a Vocation' in H.H. Gerth and C.W. Mills (eds), *From Max Weber: Essays in Sociology* (Routledge 2007) 78.

25 Elies van Sliedregt, 'International Criminal Law: Over-studied and Underachieving?' 29 *Leiden Journal of International Law* 1.

26 Robert J. Currie, *An Introduction to Transnational Criminal Law.(Book review)* (2015) 13 *Journal of International Criminal Justice* 1166.

its formal frameworks.[27] This scholarship has highlighted the design of international criminal law mechanisms to suppress private crimes carried out by individuals or groups (natural or legal individuals) for specific gains that are themselves influenced by the development of illegal markets across borders.

Transnational criminal law consists in a formal legal sense of the laws and rules spelled out in the legal instruments created to regulate criminal justice approaches to these crimes. It is an inherently dualistic system in which the state maintains the right to criminalise, but becomes a party to conventions or adopt other international instruments that ensure bilateral or multilateral criminalisation of certain crimes. This process in effect transnationalises criminal justice responses to said crimes. This system has both horizontal obligations between states and vertical commitments of individual states to live up to their treaty obligations. In terms of substantive law, the criminal offences codified in these instruments do not in necessarily transgress national borders, but most are aimed at suppressing specific forms of behavior or activities deemed problematic because they can potentially have spillover effects from one state to the next. In terms of procedural law, many of these instruments feature articles that aim to create more effective cooperation between national criminal justice systems in the form of setting up contact points for dealing with specific offences, mechanisms for international law enforcement cooperation, rules and procedures for formal legal assistance as well as for extradition. The dualistic nature of this system means that national states remain at its core. Questions of the effectiveness, legitimacy and transparency of this system must be analyzed at different levels of governance at which it is administered by specific bureaucracies of legal experts[28] affected by the development

27 Robert John Currie, *International and transnational criminal law* (Irwin Law 2010); Neil Boister and Robert J. Currie, *Routledge handbook of transnational criminal law* (Routledge, Taylor & Francis Group 2015); Wui Ling Cheah, 'Fair treatment in transnational and international criminal law' 25 *Singapore Academy of Law Journal* 778; David Luban, Julie R. O'Sullivan and David P. Stewart, *International and transnational criminal law* (Aspen Law & Business 2010); Sabine Gless and J.A.E. Vervaele, 'Law Should Govern: Aspiring General Principles for Transnational Criminal Justice' 9 *Utrecht Law Review* 1; Alejandro Chehtman, 'Terrorism and the Conceptual Divide between International and Transnational Criminal Law' in Harmen van der Wilt (ed), *Legal Responses to Transnational and International Crimes: Towards an Integrative Approach?* (Edward Elgar 2017) 107; Sadiq Reza, 'Transnational Criminal Law and Procedure: An Introduction' (2006) 56 *Journal of Legal Education* 430.

28 Mikkel Jarle Christensen, 'International Prosecution and National Bureaucracy: The Contest to Define International Practices within the Danish Prosecution Service' *Law & Social Inquiry* DOI: 10.1111/lsi.12254, accessed 10 November 2017.

of particular legal norms.[29] This structuration is in many ways inscribed in the formal legal frameworks that focuses on creating criminal justice expertise to deal with specific crimes. Due to the esoteric nature of specialised criminal justice expertise and professional power at the national and international level, understanding the development of transnational criminal law necessitates studies of the social structure of this space.

The social structure of transnational criminal law is the third dimension investigated by the articles in this special issue. The deeper social structurations of this space are of crucial importance; the strategies and practices devised here mark the embodiment of specific conceptual schemas of which concrete professionals are the main bearers and promotors. In other words, the perception of transnational crime as a problem of international concern cannot only be studied at the level of high politics. It is constructed and circulated among a range of stakeholders at national, regional and international levels each of whom tries to shape it according to their own concepts of how it ought to function. While some of these stakeholders have roots in institutions and organizations that go back almost a century, others emerged after the end of the Cold War and have worked for decades to raise specific crimes to the political agenda both nationally and internationally. From these domestic platforms, they have entered into transnational networks to support their work when more traditional paths to influence were blocked. In the struggle to define which crimes are to be given attention, the push for transnationalisation has come from very different sources. In some cases international criminal justice experts[30] in, for instance, Interpol or Europol, have helped create new forms of legal cooperation and practices, while in others, international NGOs such as Transparency International (TI) have played crucial roles as innovators and promotors of specific norms and as drivers in the evolution of new global prohibition regimes.[31] In the space of transnational criminal law, the role of law enforcement professionals, in particular, has garnered attention.[32] These pro-

29 See Rose (n 19).

30 Didier Bigo, 'Sociology of Transnational Guilds' 10 International Political Sociology 398; Antoine Mégie, 'The origin of EU authority in criminal matters: a sociology of legal experts in European policy-making' [Routledge] 21 *Journal of European Public Policy* 230.

31 Ethan A. Nadelmann, 'Global prohibition regimes: the evolution of norms in international society' 44 *International Organization* 479.

32 James Sheptycki, 'Critical reflections on transnational crime and transnational police' 47 *Criminologie* 13; James Sheptycki and Benjamin Bowling, *Policing the Caribbean: Transnational Security Cooperation in Practice* (Oxford University Press 2010); Peter Andreas and Ethan Avram Nadelmann, *Policing the globe: criminalization and crime control in international relations* (Oxford University Press 2006); Ethan Avram Nadelmann,

fessionals are crucial as they build up both specialized expertise working with specific crimes and more general competences that can translate into policy building at the national, regional and international level. As such they can be said to be at the center of the programmatic development of a transnational criminal law in which crime fighting technologies and perceptions are characterized by specific fields of stakeholders. This opens central questions as to the position of concrete institutions, networks and agents in the larger space focused on transnational crime, more particularly about how the balance between different stakeholders involved in the definition and administration of the criminal justice response to a specific crime affects the symbolic and material practices developed around this response. This perspective does not render politics or law obsolete. On the contrary, the goal is to develop a viewpoint that shows how politics are conducted across a variety of stakeholders and how this field of agents affects the development and administration of the transnational criminal law.

II Structure of the Special Issue

The special issue follows the analytical dimensions defined above. Kicking off the special issue, Neil Boister revisits and refines his previous work through an investigation of the workings of different forms of international cooperation against transnational crime, in a trans-national political space. Using historical examples, Boister explores how transnational criminal law is used as a tool that can create a legal space within the state where a fugitive resides or is acting, in order effectively to re-set the border inside that jurisdiction and to make it possible, by proxy, to enforce another state's law. Analysing the frameworks around a legal technology that is both crucial and emblematic for transnational criminal justice, the article shows how this form of law is used to establish a fictional legal space that minimises restrictions in cooperative action. With this problem in mind the article does two things: It explores how that space is created and how it shapes the structure of transnational criminal law through the building of normative structures—both legal and administrative—to suppress the activities of alleged criminals in this space. But relying on the insights of Walter Benjamin among others, its specific focus is on how this purely functional relationship impacts negatively on the human rights of 'bad global

---

Cops across borders, the internationalization of U.S. criminal law enforcement (0271010940, Pennsylvania State University Press 1993); Saskia Hufnagel and Carole McCartney, *Trust in International Police and Justice Cooperation* (Bloomsbury Publishing PLC 2017).

citizens' caught within that space, and suggests a more principled approach to the development of these laws.

Cecily Rose investigates why the system of transnational criminal law lacks the monitoring mechanisms that characterise other fields of transnational law. The article examines possible explanations for this lack of monitoring mechanisms and explores the significance of their absence from a compliance perspective. Focusing on the legal characteristics and potential impact of monitoring mechanisms, Rose analyses a number of possible explanations for their absence in transnational criminal law. These explanations range from the potentially burdensome and duplicative character of monitoring mechanisms, which states may care to avoid, to the fact that the treaties negotiated in this space are inherently less forward-looking than, for example, international environmental law treaties. In addition to these dynamics, historical factors are investigated and linked to the diversity and decentralised character of the transnational criminal law field. The field lacks a true geographical or institutional center that might foster the spread of certain trends, such as treaty monitoring bodies. The article does not discount the possibility that states have deliberately refrained from creating monitoring bodies due to a reluctance or disinterest in ensuring compliance with treaties that can have profound implications for domestic criminal justice systems. While not advocating the implementation of monitoring mechanisms in this space of law, Rose shows how their absence shapes the structure of transnational criminal law and justice and, perhaps more troubling, formats the scholarship of its practices.

James Sheptycki analyses the historical and professional development of a specific legal technology: Interpol's Red Notices. The article demonstrates how the Interpol organisation constituted itself into a formal 'Intergovernmental Organization' with its own self-governing structure and explores the use of one of its most powerful legal tools. Following Terence C. Halliday and Gregory Shaffer, but adding an original empirical case study, the article argues that Interpol is a constituent element in a broader 'transnational legal order' of global policing, a constitutive element in transnational criminal justice. This insight necessitates an analysis of the social structuration of this space and the legal and political strategies developed within it. Transnational legal orders involve a variety of actors using different kinds of legal instruments and the institutional patterns of this space have consequences for future developments. The example of Interpol as a transnational organisation reveals one element of a much bigger transnational legal order that has no democratic oversight and which can only be glimpsed at in piecemeal empirical case studies. However, read against the backdrop of broader socio-historical evolution of law such case studies offer unusual insights about contemporary legal ordering.

Finally, using sociological tools and concepts, Mikkel Jarle Christensen contributes an analysis of the social structure of transnational criminal justice. The main goal of his analysis is to investigate if the terminology crafted around transnational criminal law as a distinct legal system corresponds to the social structuration of this space as it can be observed in the practices that constitute it. To enable such an analysis, the article contributes both a theoretical discussion of how to conceptualise the social space of transnational as well as, more cautiously, an empirical investigation into the workings of this space. The latter part of the inquiry focuses on four different corners of transnational criminal law: drug trafficking, terrorism, corruption and ecological crimes. Building on Pierre Bourdieu's field theory, he analyses the subject matter of transnational criminal law and the professionals active in this space. With a foundation four separate areas of practice that are related to the two different fields of security and governance, the article offers a critical perspective on the social practices that constitute this space of law as well as on the theoretical understanding of how transnational criminal justice is structured.

The 'Bad Global Citizen', 'Naked', in the 'Transnational Penal Space'

*Neil Boister**
School of Law, University of Canterbury, New Zealand
neil.boister@canterbury.ac.nz

Abstract

This article explores how transnational criminal law is used as a tool to create a legal space within the state where the fugitive resides or is acting, in order in effect to re-set the border inside that jurisdiction and to make it possible, by proxy, to enforce another state's law. It argues that transnational criminal law is used to establish a kind of fictional transnational legal space, created by changing domestic laws and practices of both the state exercising its jurisdiction and the state in which that jurisdiction is being exercised, so that restrictions on cooperative action are minimalized. It explores how that space is created and how it shapes the structure of transnational criminal law through the building of normative structures—both legal and administrative—to suppress the activities of alleged criminals in this space. But its specific focus is on how this purely functional relationship impacts on individuals caught within that space.

Keywords

transnational criminal law – transnational penal space – cosmopolitan citizens – bad global citizen

Introduction

Suppression of transnational crime (in the sense of crime that crosses borders as opposed to fugitives who commit crimes domestically and then flee

* My thanks to my co-editor Mikkel Christensen and the anonymous reviewer for their very useful comments.

 | DOI 10.1163/9789004365797_003

abroad)[1] sits uncomfortably with the deeply held orthodox legal position that criminal justice, even in response to transnational crime, is territorially bounded. The fundamental problem in responding to cross-border crime has always been the nature of the relationship between State A and individuals located in State B who engage in activities that State A seeks to suppress because they disturb its peace.[2] Historically, the way in which transnational criminal law has been structured, both in a strictly legal and in a political sense, has been shaped by attempts to resolve the conflicting sovereign interests thrown up by this problem of extraterritoriality. For example, when in 1931 the League of Nations Fifth Committee produced a lengthy report for the League Assembly on 'the possible intensification of the war upon crime through international cooperation',[3] Kuhn commented:[4]

> The crux of the problem is that the divergences of law and procedure be fully recognized and yet that the administration of criminal police and criminal justice be coordinated throughout the world by a full exchange of information, by active cooperation in apprehending criminals, and in a logical and just division among the various countries of their sovereign jurisdiction to punish for crime.

His view of the necessity for international coordination of jurisdiction and cooperation in enforcement is unsurprising; he gave it five years after the Permanent Court of International Justice had recognized that the enforcement of jurisdiction is restricted by the sovereign equality of states in the *Lotus* Case.[5]

---

1 Although many of the same problems are encountered by cross border criminality and criminals who flee across borders, the latter situation is less complicated because it only throws up problems of the enforcement of territorial jurisdiction, rather than of the establishment and enforcement of extra-territorial jurisdiction.

2 M. Dubber, 'Criminal Jurisdiction and Conceptions of Penality in Comparative Perspective' 63 *University of Toronto law Journal* (2013) 247, 249. For a definition of transnational criminal law see Boister, 'Transnational Criminal Law?' 14 EJIL (2003) 953; 'Further Reflections on the Concept of Transnational Criminal Law' 6(1) *Transnational Legal Theory* (2015) 9.

3 League of Nations, Gradual Unification of Criminal Laws and Cooperation of States in the Prevention of and Suppression of Crime, Official Series of the League of Nations Publications No. 7 (Geneva: League of Nations, 1933).

4 Arthur Kuhn, 'International Cooperation in the Suppression of Crime' (1934) 28(3) *American Journal of International Law* 541, 542.

5 (1927) PCIJ Reports Series A No. 10, 18–20.

The reality of globalisation today challenges the bounded nature of law enforcement even more than it did in the 1930s. It is characterised in the benign sense by a world in which 'global citizens', citizens of everywhere, are no longer focussed on their rights qua that State but rather on their rights in all States. In a malign sense, 'bad global citizens' control the flow of people and contraband across borders in a way that presents a problem for territorially bounded criminal law. States 'harden' their borders with increased security and state-of-the-art technology, but as Rumford notes,

> ... they are largely unable to prevent ... the movement of illegal immigrants, terrorists, traffickers in people and drugs or whosever is deemed to represent a threat at any particular time: those beyond borders are no longer in awe of them.[6]

The standard solution to combating cross-border crime today remains largely the same as that used in the 1930s: transnational crime can only be met by one criminal justice system cooperating with another.[7] A state acting alone cannot succeed in suppressing serious threats from non-state actors beyond its borders, so states must cooperate out of mutual interest, as a matter of

---

6 Chris Rumford, 'Theorizing Borders' 9(2) *European Journal of Social Theory* (2006) 155, 156–7.

7 Supranational institutions such as the International Criminal Court are distinguishable from national implementation of cross border crimes because they are devoted to the application of 'individual' criminal responsibility under international law to 'the most serious crimes of concern to the international community as a whole'—see article 25 and article 5(1) of the Rome Statute of the International Criminal Court, 17 July 1998, 2187 UNTS 90; in force 1 July 2002. Supranational regional institutions such as that currently under development in the EU and in the Criminal Chamber of the African Court of Human Rights (see C. Jalloh, K. Clarke and V. Mehielle (eds), *The African Court of Justice and Human and Peoples' Rights in Context* (forthcoming CUP, 2018)) provide for the partial/potential elevation of institutional responsibility to a regional level, and thus point to the easing of the enforcement burden on states. So to do global developments such as the World Bank's anti-corruption mechanisms (see generally World Bank Office of Suspension and Disbarment, *Report on Functions Data and Lessons Learned 2007–2015, second edition*, Washington: World Bank, 2015, available at <http://siteresources.worldbank.org/EXTOFFEVASUS/Resources/OSDReport.pdf> last visited 9 November 2017) which investigate allegations of corruption in the award of World Bank funded projects, and which can lead to sanctions such as debarment of companies operating transnationally. However, the enforcement of criminal sanctions generally remains the preserve of the State.

international necessity.[8] As the Supreme Court of Canada put it in *Libman v Queen*,[9] '[i]n a shrinking world, we are all our brother's keepers'.

The maintenance of exclusive sovereign control is a precept of international cooperation against crime. Yet oddly, if examined more closely, in response to the failure of these borders to keep criminals and contraband out, the legal boundaries between the states concerned appear to become more indistinct. Criminal law appears to flow across borders in pursuit of these criminals. To give an example, someone located outside the United States might cross the border into the United States simply by making a key-stoke on the keyboard of their computer. Through the operation of the US's extraterritorial jurisdiction they may become a fugitive[10] from US justice while sitting at their desk, even though they have never been to the United States. That does not mean, however, that the FBI will come bursting through their door to arrest them. What is more likely is that in the process of cooperating the state in which they reside will come under pressure to accommodate US interests and gradually soften its strict legal requirements to make it possible to get information about that person, and perhaps eventually that person, into US jurisdiction. In strict legal terms that state applies its own law on behalf of the US; but to the individual involved it can feel like they are being subject, even if only indirectly, to US law, and there is a perception of the blurring of jurisdictional boundaries. British MP (later Attorney General) Dominic Grieve's comment on the relaxation of extradition relations between the UK and the other member states of the European Union under the European Arrest Warrant[11] and with the United States under the 2003 US-UK Extradition Treaty[12] is illustrative of this unease: in his view this relaxation betrayed 'an extraordinary internationalism and an

---

8 Erin Creegan, 'A Permanent Hybrid Court for Terrorism' (2011) 26 *American University International Law Review* 237, 246–51.

9 [1985] 2 SCR 178, 214.

10 In terms of the US Fugitive Disentitlement Statute 28 USC § 2466 a person is a fugitive not only if they purposefully leave US criminal jurisdiction to avoid apprehension but if they decline to enter or renter it, or otherwise evade its jurisdiction.

11 Council Framework Decision on the European Arrest Warrant and the Surrender Procedures between Member States of the European Union of 13 June 2002 OJ L 190/1, 18 July 2002, in force 1 January 2004.

12 Extradition Treaty between the Government of the United States of America and the Government of the United Kingdom of Great Britain and Northern Ireland, 31 March 2003, UST 108–23.

attitude that state borders are rather archaic with a reluctance to stand up for their own.'[13]

This article explores how transnational criminal law can be used to create legal spaces within the state where a fugitive resides or is acting, in order in practical effect to re-set the border inside that jurisdiction and to make it possible, by proxy, to enforce another state's law. It argues that transnational criminal law is used to establish what can be characterised as a fictional 'transnational legal space', created by changing domestic laws and practices of both the state exercising its jurisdiction and the state in which that jurisdiction is being exercised, so that restrictions on cooperative action are minimalized. In an echo of the erratic appearance of these spaces, it draws on an eclectic range of examples from different prohibition regimes, different national laws and different cases within transnational criminal law to explore how that space can be created, how it can shape the structure of transnational criminal law through the building of normative structures—both legal and administrative—to suppress the activities of alleged criminals in this space, and how this purely functional relationship can have a negative impact on individuals caught within that space. It does so, first in Part One by outlining the problem of policing the 'bad global citizen'. Part Two explores the mechanics for the creation of a transnational penal space. Part Three describes how the legal response through transnational criminal law can leave the rights of 'bad global citizens' unprotected and open to abuse. Part Four engages in a theoretical exploration of how, metaphorically speaking, the 'bad global citizen' is stripped 'naked' in that space. Part Five speculates as to what can be done to re-clothe the 'bad global citizen'. Finally, the conclusion examines theoretical justifications as to why it is important to do so.

1 The Transnational Criminal as a 'Bad Global Citizen'

Philosophers from Rousseau to Rawls place the good citizen at the centre of liberal political arrangements. These good citizens bear their obligations and exercise their rights within the law of nation states. They enjoy status in their communities, communities to which they owe allegiance. Conceptions of the nature of this citizenship vary widely. Rousseau famously argues that humans

13 *Hansard*, 12 July 2006 col 1419, cited in Asif Efrat, 'Resisting Cooperation against Crime: Britain's Extradition Controversy, 2003–2015' (2017) *International Journal of Law, Crime and Justice* 17, available online at <https://doi.org/10.1016/j.ijlcj.2017.10.004> last visited 10 November 2017.

living in a society must reconcile their own sense of subjective freedom with the objective need to act correctly.[14] Less coercively Rawls argues that citizens have the capacity to pursue their own conception of what is good and share a conception of primary goods such as the basic liberties within a society defined by fairness.[15] Citizenship, though, is conceived of as exercised within the nation state.

Whether notional equivalents to this national citizenship exist at a global level has been a subject of debate for some time.[16] For Falk, the rationalist-elitist embodiment of this notion can be described as follows:

> [T]he global citizen as a type of global reformer: an individual who intellectually perceives a better way of organizing the political life of the planet, and favors a utopian scheme that is presented as a practical mechanism.[17]

This idealised concept of global citizenship contrasts with the parochial reality of the transnational global citizen doing business (whether it be commercial, governmental, moral or whatever) in different places, connected, networked, and expectant of a certain minimum level of treatment from the state in which they may currently find themselves or in which their interests may currently be engaged. This reality is more aptly described by Somek's[18] view of cosmopolitan citizens as de-nationalised individuals free to associate and move trans-nationally and claiming rights to equal treatment irrespective of nationality. Whatever the particular conception of global citizenship, they all share a completely de-territorialised concept of citizenship. Yet the simple political reality of state monopolies on power within their domain reserve means that the State as an institution still interposes itself between individuals and a global society of individuals.

This interposition of state authority is particularly evident in regard to the treatment of those whose trans-national actions deliberately flout the law,

---

14 Jean Jacques Rosseau, *The Social Contract*, (London: Penguin edn, 1968), chapters 5–8.

15 John Rawls, *Justice as Fairness* (Cambridge, Mass: Harvard UP, 2001), Part 1.

16 See generally Daniele Archibugi, *The Global Commonwealth of Citizens: Toward Cosmopolitan Democracy* (Princeton and Oxford: Princeton UP, 2008); Jeffrey L. Dunoff and Joel P. Trachtman (eds.), *Ruling The World: International Law, Global Governance, Constitutionalism* (Cambridge: CUP, 2009).

17 Richard Falk, 'The Making of Global Citizenship' in J. Brecher, J.B. Childs and J. Cutler (eds.) *Global Visions: Beyond the New World Order* (Boston: South End, 1993), 39, 42.

18 *The Cosmopolitan Constitution* (Oxford: OUP, 2014), 205 et seq.

individuals who share a sense of how to profit from actions that others consider 'bad'[19] both in a moral and legal sense. Pirates, slavers, drug traffickers, corrupters, human traffickers, people smugglers, terrorists, organised criminals, money launderers, cybercriminals, environmental criminals, weapons traffickers, illicit traffickers in cultural property, organ traffickers, fraudsters, counterfeiters, identity thieves, or criminals of other ilk, may through their cross-border actions become subject to the substantive criminal jurisdiction of more than one state. Networking with other criminals across borders usually for some form of personal gain, they engage, as Falk terms it,[20] in a kind of globalisation 'from below'.

Justice Oliver Wendell Holmes wryly noted that 'if you want to know the law and nothing else, you must look at it as a bad man, who cares only for the material consequences which such knowledge enables him to predict.'[21] The 'bad' woman or man who traffics (or engages in some other activity) across borders is concerned about the laws in the states in which they operate because avoiding these laws represents an external cost to their criminal activity. Relying on secrecy, corruption, or coercion, or the simple fact that one state criminalizes an activity but another does not (either on paper or in practice),[22] they try to create and exploit what can be termed 'transnational criminal spaces', the spaces where national legal systems cease to be effective, in order to commit injurious actions. Lawmakers and enforcement officials in their turn, seek ways to suppress the actions of these transnational criminals effectively, and in doing so exploit the fact that these criminals may be operating beyond the reach of domestic laws restraining executive action.

---

19 The loaded language with which they are described is common across the range of offences—Somali pirates, for example, are 'bloodthirsty and merciless' (Osiro (n 69), 4), while drug traffickers are 'engineers of evil' (The Malaysian Chief Justice cited in Sidney L. Harrington, 'Death, Drugs and Development: Malaysia's Mandatory Death Penalty for Traffickers and the International War on Drugs' (1991) 29 *Columbia Journal of Transnational Law* 365, 380)—which plays a role in the process of redefinition of criminals as morally and then through legislative intervention legally deviant—see Peter Andreas and Ethan Nadelmann, *Policing the Globe: Criminalization and Crime Control in International Relations* (Oxford: OUP, 2006), 6.

20 Falk (n 17), 39.

21 Oliver Wendell Holmes Jr, 'The Path of the Law' (1897) 10 *Harvard Law Review* 457.

22 Raymond J. Michalowski and Ronald C. Kramer, 'The Space between Laws: The Problem of Corporate Crime in a Transnational Context' (1987) 34 (1) *Social Problems* 34, 36, define the space between laws as the space between actions permissible in one country but prohibited in another.

II The Mechanics of Creating a Transnational Penal Space

This process of enforcing the law in 'transnational criminal spaces' bears a certain resemblance to the ancient response to certain kinds of criminals that deliberately placed them outside the law by outlawing them.

> According to the ancient English concept of outlawry: 'he who breaks the law has gone to war with the community; the community goes to war with him. It is the right and duty of every man to pursue him, to ravage his land, to burn his house, to hunt him down like a wild beast and slay him; for a wild beast he is; not merely is he a "friendless man", he is a wolf.'[23]

Since the Nineteenth Century, states have responded in a more restrained way to extraterritorial crime by adopting 'rules and legal instruments … specifically created to deal with transnational criminal matters'.[24] They have treated transnational criminals as the objects of collaboration with other states, and adopted a range of different kinds of legal instruments for this purpose. These include bilateral and regional extradition and legal assistance conventions, such as the highly influential 1957 European Extradition Convention.[25] Global crime suppression conventions like the UN Convention against Transnational Organised Crime[26] (UNTOC), have also been used to standardise crimes at the national level and further enable international cooperation in the investigation, extradition and prosecution of transnational criminals. The Security Council has weighed in with binding measures such as Resolution 2178[27] on foreign fighters, which requires UN Member states to take essentially preventive measures against potential transnational criminals. Soft laws, such as the Financial Action Tasks Force's International Standards on Combating Money Laundering and the Financing of Terrorism and Proliferation,[28] have been used

---

23 Note, 'The Disenfranchisement of Ex-Felons: Citizenship, Criminality, and the "Purity" of the Ballot Box' (1989) 102 *Harvard Law Review* 1300, 1301, n 6.

24 Sabine Gless and John A. Vervaele, 'Editorial: Law Should Govern: Aspiring General Principles for Transnational Criminal Justice' (2013) 9 *Utrecht Law Review* 1, 3.

25 12 December 1957, ETS 24, in force 18 April 1960. See also the Additional Protocol to the European Convention, 15 October 1975, ETS 86, in force 20 August 1979; Second Additional Protocol to the European Convention, 17 March 1978, ETS 98, in force 5 June 1983.

26 The United Nations Convention against Transnational Organized Crime, 15 November 2000, 2225 UNTS 209, in force 29 September 2003.

27 Resolution 2178, 24 September 2014.

28 FATF, 2012, available at <http://www.fatf-gafi.org/publications/fatfrecommendations/documents/fatf-recommendations.html> last visited 10 November 2017.

to provide for a much tougher sanctions backed implementation regime than more formal treaty obligations. In recent years we have seen a proliferation of new regimes such as counterfeiting of medicine[29] and the smuggling of tobacco,[30] and moves towards suppression of piracy of intellectual property on the internet.[31]

There is no single point of origin for the highly complex plural system of transnational criminal laws that has resulted. Its multiple points of origin include the unilateral domestic actions of states, or agreements between states, or may even arise out of the actions of IGOs or companies (such as the banks engaged in self-regulation for anti-money laundering purposes). The single nexus all of these rules have, however, is a focus on cross-border crime. A number of general features characterise this response. First, the State generally retains the right to penalise. Second, these instruments rest on the policy-making assumption that an increase in the exercise of state authority over these transnational criminals is in the best interests of all.

These legal instruments serve to overcome the legal limitations imposed on enforcement of jurisdiction by territorial borders. Territorial borders are an expression of modernity; they emerged in the post Westphalian era as an incident of territorial sovereignty.[32] Borders still matter to the modern state as they delineate the outer limits of legal enforcement action against crime. In order to reach beyond these borders, 'transnational penal spaces'[33] have had to be created to suppress the actions of individuals who might be called 'bad global citizens'. One may well imagine that these 'transnational penal spaces' are inter-sovereign spaces, somewhere between borders, relatively free of legal protection. Yet they are always legally speaking 'somewhere'; the individual concerned is always in a territory or plane or on a ship under the at least

29 See the Council of Europe Convention on the counterfeiting of medical products and similar crimes involving threats to public health (or MEDICRIME convention), 28 October 2011, CETS No. 211.

30 See Conference of the Parties to the WHO Framework Convention on Tobacco Control, Protocol to Eliminate Illicit Trade in Tobacco Products, 12 November 2012, FCTC COP/5/6, 11 May 2012.

31 See G. Urbas, 'Copyright, Crime and Computers: New Legislative Frameworks for Intellectual Property Rights Enforcement' (2012) 7 *Journal of International Commercial Law and Technology* 11.

32 Kalevi J. Holsti, *Taming the Sovereigns: Institutional Change in International Politics* (Cambridge: CUP, 2004) 73.

33 On the general theory of transnational spaces see Craig Scott, '"Transnational Law" as Proto-Concept: Three Conceptions' 10 *German Law Journal* (2009) 859, 873–875; Harold H. Koh, 'Transnational Legal Process' (1996) 75 *Nebraska Law Review* 181, 199.

nominal legal control of a State. It is more accurate to say they are intra- sovereign spaces where the domestic jurisdiction, notionally exclusive, gives way to the interests of the State pursing the criminal extra-territorially whether legally or simply practically.

Creating a 'transnational legal space' begins with the establishment of an extraterritorial jurisdiction that is based on some kind of nexus with the state's interests. The establishment of this jurisdiction may be explicit[34] or implied from the nature of a particular domestic law or statute in an unexceptionable manner so long as it conforms to recognised general principles of extraterritorial jurisdiction.[35] States may, however, sometimes extend their long enforcement arm abroad without apparent legislative authority and in ways that appear to reach beyond any formally sanctioned and reasonable jurisdictional interest. The high seas have provided a particularly rich opportunity for questionable assertions of extra-territorial jurisdiction despite sovereign control over flag vessels. Clark explores a number of Eighteenth and Nineteenth century examples where in practice Great Britain, then global policeman, acting in terms of bilateral treaties appeared to enforce a jurisdiction over slave-trading on the high seas that it had not previously established.[36] In a more recent example of such an unauthorised enforcement activity, Kontorovich shows how the US in the Maritime Drug Law Enforcement Act[37] extended and enforced universal jurisdiction without constitutional warrant over drug traffickers on the high seas who are not US citizens, not on US vessels and not heading towards the US.[38] Article I of the US Constitution grants power over piracy on the high seas because the high seas were outside of the jurisdiction of any state; in pursuit of a general global police power, the US analogised drug trafficking with piracy without meeting the requirement that the exercise of universal jurisdiction must be applied to offences recognised by the law of nations—i.e. core international crimes.

---

34 See, among the many thousands of domestic examples, article 6 of Iceland's Penal Code which *inter alia* expressly gives Iceland extraterritorial jurisdiction regardless of nationality over a broad range of transnational crimes.

35 First spelled out pithily in the Harvard Draft Convention on Jurisdiction with Respect to Crime, (1935) 29 AJIL 439.

36 See Roger Clark, 'Some Aspects of the Concept of International Criminal Law: Suppression Conventions, Jurisdiction, Submarine Cables and the Lotus' (2011) 22 *Criminal Law Forum* 519, 524–5.

37 Codified at 46 USC § 70501–70507.

38 Eugene Kontorovich, 'Beyond the Article I Horizon: Congress's Enumerated Powers and Universal Jurisdiction Over Drug Crimes' (2009) 93 *Minnesota Law Review* 1191, 1195 et seq.

Direct enforcement of prescribed extraterritorial jurisdiction in another state's territory is not possible in other states, however, without their cooperation, because as noted, the orthodox position on the enforcement of jurisdiction is that the sovereign's authority within its territory is absolute and it must consent to any exception to that authority.[39] States rely on various modes of international cooperation—direct information exchange, specific modes of transnational police cooperation, mutual legal assistance, extradition, prisoner transfer, asset forfeiture—to enforce their extraterritorial jurisdiction. While formally this involves an exercise in the exclusive domestic authority of the state that is requested to provide assistance, inevitably it involves a compromise on the exclusivity of domestic authority. Thus, for example, while a number of Caribbean states have signed 'shiprider' agreements allowing one of their officials based on board a US vessel to sanction such enforcement, asserting their sovereignty others initially resisted consenting to such extraterritorial enforcement in their own territorial waters.[40] Interestingly, Brown identifies the origins of these agreements in nineteenth and twentieth century law enforcement cooperation treaty precedents governing inter alia piracy and slave-trading at sea.[41]

Extradition is an important tool for creating a transnational legal space in pursuit of the enforcement of extraterritorial jurisdiction. The orthodox position is that when it comes to decision on whether to order surrender, the *lex fori* governs. However, that is not the way a fugitive experiences the foreign sovereign's power—to them and to third party observers, indeed even to the territorial sovereign itself, extradition can feel like the exercise of *imperium in imperio*, a sovereign acting within a sovereign, mainly because the *lex fori* has to give ground in order to make extradition work. The origins of many of the compromises in modern extradition law lie in US practice in regard to fugitives fleeing from the US to Mexico in the later quarter of the nineteenth century, when the US built its hegemonic power not only through war and trade but as Margolies put its 'in the spaces of law'.[42] He illustrates how even during this pe-

---

39 *Schooner Exchange v McFaddon* 11 US (7 Cranch) 116 (1812).

40 See Hilbourne Watson, 'The Shiprider Solution and Post-Cold War imperialism: Beyond Ontologies of State Sovereignty in the Caribbean' in Cynthia Barrow-Giles and Don M. Marshall, *Living at the Borderlines: Issues in Caribbean Sovereignty and Development* (Kinsgton: Ian Randle, 2003), 226.

41 Kathy-Ann Brown, *The Shiprider Model: an analysis of the U.S. proposed* agreement *concerning maritime counter-drug operations in its wider legal context* (Bridgetown, Barbados University of the West Indies, 2007) 1–2.

42 D.S. Margolies, *Spaces of Law in American Foreign Relations: Extradition and Extraterritoriality in the Borderlands and Beyond, 1877–1898* (Athens GA: University of Georgia Press, 2011), 4.

riod of strongly asserted territorial sovereignty, extradition was used to pursue unilateral governance of transnational problems. This involved US authorities pressuring Mexico to create accommodating spaces in its law through sovereign exception, at the same time as they pushed for the insertion of sovereign exceptions into their own law when transnational jurisdictional issues were involved. Margolies notes:

> The system of extradition relationships as created by treaty and exercised by the executive branch was an aspect of foreign policy in which state power was designed to be relatively autonomous of the rule of law it was serving.[43]

A modern analogy might be found in regard to the controversy surrounding the UK's unequal extradition relationship with the US based in recent years, based around the one-sided nature of the obligations in the 2003 US-UK Extradition Treaty. One example serves to illustrate: Gary McKinnon, whose extradition was requested by the US to face computer hacking charges, was told in the US embassy in London that if he made a guilty plea to the charges he would get back home, with the implication that if he fought extradition and pleaded innocent, he would not.[44]

Compromises of this kind are not unique to extradition. US law enforcement agencies such as the Drug Enforcement Administration pursued the creation of transnational legal spaces in the area of police cooperation in the 20th Century by taking procedures first piloted domestically such as controlled delivery, and then trialling them in a transnational context in Latin America and Europe.[45] The DEA succeeded in this role because it operated vicariously through local police agencies rather than attempting to expand its own freedom of operation, and by ensuring that local policing laws and practices harmonized with its own.[46]

Again it is not simply a case of the territorial state giving way. The creation of these spaces necessitates compromise within the domestic law of the state that is operating extraterritorially. This point is well illustrated by a recent US

43 Ibid., 5.

44 House of Commons Home Affairs Committee, *The US-UK Extradition Treaty Twentieth Report of Session 2010–12 Volume I: Report, together with formal minutes, oral and written evidence*, HC 644, London: The Stationery Office Limited, 30 March 2012, EV 40.

45 See generally P. Andreas and E. Nadelmann, *Policing the Globe: Criminalization and Crime Control in International Relations* (Oxford: OUP, 2006), 105, 128 et seq.

46 See E. Nadelmann, *Cops Across Borders: The Internationalization of U.S. Criminal Law Enforcement* (Philadelphia, PA: Penn State University Press, 1993), 189–249.

transnational forfeiture case, the *US v Batato and others*.[47] The issue on appeal was whether the US Courts had jurisdiction to order forfeiture *in rem* when the bank accounts in question were in New Zealand and Hong Kong and required the enforcement of those orders in those countries. The standard rule of US law required the Court to have actual or constructive control of the property in question.[48] The legislature had intervened out of practical necessity in order to legally enable transnational forfeiture, by amending the forfeiture legislation to make it possible to issue process against property outside that jurisdiction.[49] The defence argued that this did not establish jurisdiction in the issuing court, only venue. A majority in the Federal Court of Appeal for the Ninth Circuit affirmed the District Court's finding that the section established jurisdiction.[50] An alternative defence argument that this amounted to the US court engaging in an impermissible advisory opinion in the sense that it was advising the courts of New Zealand and Hong Kong because the US did not have control of the *res* was also rejected, on the basis of an exception to the rule against advisory judgments because the foreign sovereigns had detained the *res* pursuant to the litigation.[51] In dissent Floyd J. noted, however, that the probability of the New Zealand courts enforcing the order was not enough; the US court could not give an order that was binding on the property because its fate was ultimately in the hands of the foreign courts. For him this made it an advisory opinion.[52] The majority appears to have been forced to engage in a flexible interpretation of US law so that reliance could be placed on the custody of the thing by the foreign sovereign.

It is difficult to draw out common features from these various examples of 'transnational penal spaces' and they deserve more comprehensive and detailed study. It does appear, however, that driven by national law enforcement exigencies and rationalised in the pursuit of the common good,[53] international criminal cooperation against transnational crime results in the creation of the 'transnational penal spaces' with peculiar characteristics of their own.

---

47 US Court of Appeals for the Fourth Circuit, Case No. 15–1360, 12 August 2016.

48 *US v Approximately $1.67 million* 513 F.3d 991, 996 (9th Circ. 2008). The US Supreme Court denied certiorari in *US v Batato*, 2 October 2017, Docket No 16-1206.

49 28 USC § 135(b) and (d).

50 n 49, at 10 (Gregory and Duncan JJ).

51 n 49, at 15.

52 n 49, at 54–5.

53 See, for example, preambular para 9 of the International Convention for the Financing of Terrorism, New York, 9 December, 1999, 2178 UNTS 197, in force 10 April 2002: '*Considering* that the financing of terrorism is a matter of grave concern to the international community as a whole'.

The transnational scope of investigation, prosecution, institutions engaged, and foreignness in which all this takes place, are common features of these spaces.[54] Moreover, more than accommodation, the creation of these spaces requires the erosion of domestic sovereignty and the distortion and weakening of domestic and international laws. The resulting 'frontierlands'[55] of law enforcement involve the recharacterisation of domestic criminal processes as a process that involves another State and thus changes its character, and in which the exclusive jurisdiction of the territorial state gives way to a functional jurisdiction.[56] Dubber explains that when states engage in international cooperation they are not expressing an autonomous power over themselves, but a heteronomous power over another sovereign.[57] Although it remains nominally sovereign, it must allow itself to be subject to the heteronomous power of the state that is doing the extraterritorial policing. This internalization of external space usually takes place within the external space of certain countries identified as sources of contraband. Transnational penal spaces are thus spaces of multi-level governance, where territorial sovereignty is eroded through international cooperation conducted on the basis of treaties, MOUs, ill-defined expectations of comity, diplomatic pressure, or simply through administrative relationships between individuals who share the same goals and respect and trust each other. These goals include securing information, evidence, and ultimately individual defendants, with the least restriction possible, in order to suppress what is considered to be the extreme danger offered by transnational crime.[58] The necessary compromises on sovereignty can range from the mildly disagreeable to the frankly unacceptable depending on its particular nature, although as commentators have begun to point out, law enforcement professionals are more likely to be accepting of them than politicians or the general populace.[59] The arrangements that result may also not be entirely familiar to

---

54 Marianne L. Wade, 'General Principles of Transnationalised Criminal Justice? Exploratory Reflections' (2013) 9(4) *Utrecht Law Review* 165, 166.

55 See Zygmunt Baumann, *Society under Siege* (Cambridge: Polity, 2002), 88.

56 See generally Liesbet Hooghe and Gary Marks, 'Unravelling the Central State, but How? Types of Multi-level Governance' (2003) 97(2) *American Political Science Review* 233–243.

57 See generally Dubber (n 2), 249 et seq.

58 See, for example, the US National Security Council's *Strategy to Combat Transnational Organized Crime: addressing Converging Threats to National Security* (Washington, 2011), page 5: 'Transnational organized crime (TOC) poses a significant and growing threat to national and international security, with dire implications for public safety, public health, democratic institutions, and economic stability across the globe.'

59 See generally Efrat (n 13); William Magnuson, 'The Domestic Politics of International Extradition' (2012) 52(4) *Virginia Journal of International Law* 839–901.

those directly caught up in that space; indeed, implicit in their nature as spaces of policing, these 'transnational penal spaces' may provide diminished legal protection for them.

III The 'Bad Global Citizen', 'Naked' in the 'Transnational Penal Space'

Linked, if sometimes uncomfortably, in order to ensure cooperation in suppression of crime in the 'transnational penal space', jurisdictions may be disconnected in relation to the protection of human rights who find themselves with that space. For example, in the *US v Batato*[60] the defence argued that they were not getting the protection promised in article 16 of the UNTOC (to which both the US and New Zealand are parties) of a 'guarantee of fair treatment at all stages of the proceedings including enjoyment of all the rights and guarantees provided by the domestic law of the State Party in the territory of which the person is present.' This complaint was brushed aside by the US District Court,[61] a response implicitly approved by Court of Appeal when, based upon perhaps an unwarranted degree of transnational trust in the protections afforded by the cooperating states, it commented:[62]

> That the exercise of their rights in New Zealand may cause disadvantages for the claimants with respect to litigation occurring in America does not mean they are being treated *unfairly* or that they are *denied* their enjoyment of rights in New Zealand.

When the long-arm of domestic criminal law reaches beyond territorial borders, it may also leave behind some of its domestic human rights constraints. The Canadian Supreme Court decision in *R v Hape*[63] sets out what it sees as the logic in leaving Charter protections behind in Canada when engaging in extra-territorial activity (Canadian police presence during an arrest by local enforcement officers in the Caribbean) as follows:

> Enforcement of compliance with the Charter means that when State agents act, they must do so in accordance with the requirements of the

60 n 49, at 43–4.

61 *All Assets Listed in Attachment A*, 89 F. Supp. 3d at 833.

62 n 49, at 44.

63 [2007] 2 SCR 292 at 340–1.

> Charter so as to give effect to Canadian law as it applies to the exercise of the state power at issue ... Since extraterritorial enforcement is not possible, and enforcement is necessary for the Charter to apply, extraterritorial application of the Charter is impossible.

The 'transnational penal space' may thus provide a relatively human rights free zone in which to undertake law enforcement action. The precise scope for this freedom depends on a variety of factors such as the physical location and circumstances of the enforcement activity, the identity and capacity of the enforcement agencies, and the normative strength of protections available. Abuses of the human rights of transnational criminals in the 'transnational penal space' range from mild inconsistencies with normal domestic protections such as dispensing with or severely limiting rights to discovery during extradition in many jurisdictions[64] to Lord Steyn's 'legal black holes' such as the archetypal Guantanamo Bay.[65] The tactics used by 'law enforcement' (in a loose sense) reach their most glaringly illegitimate when they engage in extraordinary rendition of suspected terrorists,[66] but these tactics build on a pedigree of unlawful surveillance, evidence-knapping, and irregular rending such as that famously legalised in the US in the *Kerr-Frisbie*.[67] My concern here, however, is not so much with these extreme examples when all reference to international law and domestic law of the territorial state is ignored, but with more commonplace activities done within the applicable international and domestic legal framework.

Some of these activities take the form of the exercise of domestic arrest powers in extraterritorial spaces, which are characterised by (i) limited local control (thus requiring cooperation) and (ii) by the limited power of the sending state to control its own enforcement authority's conduct. The interdiction and arrest of Somali pirates in the Northern Indian Ocean and Gulf of Aden has, for example, often appeared to occur in a partial legal vacuum. Pirates have been set adrift.[68] Private Military Contractors have used force in an

---

64 See, for example, M. Cherif Bassiouni, *International Extradition: United States Law and Practice* (Sixth Edition, New York: OUP, 2014), 876.

65 Johan Steyn, 'Guantanamo Bay: The Legal Black Hole' (2004) 53(1) *The International and Comparative Law Quarterly* 1–15.

66 See Leila Sadat, 'Extraordinary Rendition, Torture and Other Nightmares from the War on Terror' 75 *George Washington Law Review* (2007) 1200.

67 *Ker v Illinois* 119 US 436; *Frisbie v Collins* 342 US 519.

68 J. Peter Pham, 'Putting Somali Piracy in Context' (2010) 28 *Journal of Contemporary African Studies* 325, 332.

unregulated way against them.[69] Suspicions have been voiced that pirates may have even executed and dumped at sea.[70] Osiro notes that Western enthusiasm for enforcement action against pirates has been accompanied by a paradoxical reluctance to prosecute them domestically with full application of due process protections because of cost, distance (alleged pirates have been detained for long periods on board arresting ships awaiting a decision as to their fate[71]), the dilemmas of military involvement in law enforcement and the uncertainty of the laws on which enforcement was based.[72] Arresting powers have preferred to transfer them to regional States to prosecute (and agreements have been made to enable this[73]) even though it is not clear under the UNCLOS that this transfer of enforcement authority is permitted.[74] Commenting on the legal position of Somali Pirates before Kenyan Courts for offences alleged to have occurred on the High Seas, the High Court at Mombasa noted that

> … this court would be abdicating its jurisdiction, power and authority and its Constitutional obligations in ensuring the protection of the fundamental rights and freedoms of the [pirates] who find themselves in a perilous, insecure and unenviable situation in a strange country to which they were brought without their wish or volition.[75]

69 See generally Ved P. Nanda and Jonathan Bellish, 'Moving from Crisis Management to a Sustainable Solution for Somali Piracy: Selected initiatives and the Role of International Law' (2013) 46 *Case Western Reserve Journal of International Law* (2013) 43, 66.

70 D. Osiro, *Somali Pirates have Rights too: Judicial Consequences and Human Rights Concerns*, Institute for Security Studies Paper 224, July 2011, 1, 7 available at <https://issafrica.s3.amazonaws.com/site/uploads/Paper224SomaliPirates.pdf> last visited 9 November 2017.

71 'Amnesty Demands Dutch and Danish Take Care of Pirates' *Politiken*, 4 February 2009, available at http://www.nrc.nl/international/article2141530.ece/Amnesty_demands_Dutch_and_Danish_take_care_of_pirates.

72 Osiro (n 69), 6 ff.

73 See, for example, Exchange of Letters between the European Union and the Government of Kenya on the Conditions and Modalities for the Transfer of Persons suspected of Having Committed Acts of Piracy and Detained by the European Union-led Naval VForce (EUNAVFOR), and Seized Property in the Possession of EUNAVOR, from EUNAVFOR to Kenya and For Their Treatment after Such Transfer, 6 March 2009.

74 See M. Gardner, 'Piracy Prosecution in National Courts' (2012) 10 *Journal of International Criminal Justice* 797, 804 et seq; J. Ashley Roach, 'Countering Piracy off Somalia: International Law and International Institutions' (2010) 104 *American Journal of International Law* 397, 403.

75 Justice Mohamed Ibrahim *in re Mohamud Mohamed Hashi & 8 Others*, High Court Misc. Appl. No. 434 of 2009, 2010 eKLR 1 at 31.

Transnational police cooperation has also provided the context for the abuse of human rights. The Australian Federal Police (AFP) were unapologetic about the information they gave to Indonesian police on the activities of the drug trafficking conspiracy which led to the arrest of the 'Bali Nine' for drug trafficking in Indonesia, and eventually, after conviction to the execution of two Australian nationals who were members of the conspiracy.[76] The AFP Commissioner justified the AFP's stance out of the necessity of having to cooperate with foreign justice systems unlike that in Australia in order to take steps against transnational crime.[77] The AFP were doing precisely what article 9(2) of the 1988 UN Drug Trafficking Convention[78] obliges them to do with the enforcement authorities of other states parties, to 'co-operate with one another in conducting enquiries' with respect to drug trafficking offences in regard to the 'identity, whereabouts and activities of persons suspected of being involved in' drug trafficking offences. The general obligation to cooperate in article 9(1) is subject to consistency 'with their respective domestic legal and administrative systems' but in this instance that did not restrain the AFP's action.

Transnational criminals are perhaps most commonly exposed when subject to extradition. Human rights gains have been made in the Council of Europe and elsewhere since *Soering v United Kingdom*[79] accepted the principle that 'under international law states engage their human rights obligations when they engage in international criminal cooperation that affects an individual's fundamental human rights.'[80] Respect for human rights violations as a bar to extradition is, however, neither universally nor consistently applied. China's weak protection of human rights in its domestic criminal justice system[81] has not, for example, prevented the negotiation of extradition treaties with France and Spain, and the consideration of these treaties by New Zealand and Canada, although an Australian government attempt to get parliamentary support for ratification of the 2007 Extradition treaty it signed with China recently

76 D. Hoare, 'Australian Exceptionalism', *The Monthly*, July 2007, available at <https://www.themonthly.com.au/issue/2007/july/1283823425/daniel-hoare/australian-exceptionalism> last visited 8 November 2017.

77 Ibid.

78 Vienna, 20 December 1988, 1582 UNTS 95, in force 11 November 1990.

79 Series A, No. 161 (1989).

80 R.J. Currie, 'The Protection of Human Rights in the Suppression of Transnational Crime' in N. Boister and R.J. Currie (eds), *The Routledge Handbook of Transnational Criminal Law* (Abingdon: Routledge, 2015), 27.

81 On the extensive use for example of execution see Amnesty International Global Report, *Death Sentences and Executions 2016* (London: Amnesty International, 2017), 17.

collapsed amidst cross-party concern about potential human rights violations in China.[82]

The systems for global cooperation against transnational criminals also restructure the domestic penal space by calling for severe punishment once an individual finally gets to court. Article 3(4)(a) of the 1988 Convention requires that parties must ensure that article 3(1) offences are punished by penalties that take into account their 'grave nature', using punishments 'such as' 'imprisonment or other forms of deprivation of liberty', 'pecuniary sanctions', and 'confiscation'. Article 3(5) provides for a list of aggravating factors which may characterize an article 3(1) offence as 'particularly serious', and which parties must permit their courts to take into account. Certain states use these provisions to justify heavy punishments, in what may in some cases be a compensatory mechanism to make up for their ineffective enforcement of the full range of their treaty derived laws. For example, the only concern of the international community in regard to drug 'mules' is that they face a punishment that takes into account the 'grave nature' of the offence they have committed including by 'imprisonment'.[83] This ignores the fact that they are often subject to forms of coercion[84] or trickery[85] that would impact in particular on the voluntary nature of their conduct or mens rea, and in some situations would qualify them as being trafficked themselves.[86] Human rights bodies have criticized executions for drug offences as violations of international law,[87] but states that retain the penalty have justified it by reference to article 3(5)'s label of 'serious',

82 Jamie Smyth, 'Australia Pulls Back from China Extradition Treaty', *Financial Times*, 28 March 2017, <https://www.ft.com/content/7d70f358-1347-11e7-80f4-13e067d5072c> last visited 10 November 2017.

83 Article 3(4)(a) of the 1988 Convention.

84 UK Sentencing Council, *Drug 'Mules': Twelve Case Studies*, Office of the Sentencing Council, March, 2011, 1; Jonathan P. Caulkins, Honora Burnett and Edward Leslie, 'How Illegal Drugs Enter an Island Country: Insights From Interviews with Incarcerated Traffickers' (2009) 10 *Global Crime* 66, 84.

85 Jennifer Fleetwood, 'Five Kilos: Penalties and Practice in the International Cocaine Trade' (2011) 51 *British Journal of Criminology* 375, 380 and sources cited there; UK Sentencing Council, ibid., 4.

86 See F. Gerry et al, 'Is the Law an Ass when it comes to Mules? How Indonesia can lead a new global approach to treating drug traffickers as human trafficked victims', *Asian Journal of International Law*, 1–23, published online 4 October 2016, DOI: https://doi.org/10.1017/S2044251316000230 last visited 7 November 2017.

87 Concluding Observations of the United Nations Human Rights Committee, UN Doc CCPR/CO/84/THA, 8 July 2005, para 14, and Report of the United Nations Human Rights Committee, UN Doc A/50/40, 3 October 1995, para 449.

which they argue categorises drug trafficking as falling within the exception in article 6(2) of the International Covenant on Civil and Political Rights (ICCPR), which implicitly permits the imposition of the death penalty for the 'most serious' crimes as an exception to the right to life.[88] Human rights NGOs point out that Iran's drug interdiction programmes, supported by Western and other donors and through the UN Office of Drugs and Crime, have enabled the execution of significant numbers of convicted drug traffickers in spite of Donor State and official UN positions that condemn the use of the death penalty.[89] The UNODC and its mainly Western funders, are well aware of Iran's goal of harsh suppression of drug trafficking through execution of traffickers, but the goal of interdicting Afghan opium supply overrides any qualms the organisation or its funders may have.[90]

Another area in which the alleged transnational criminal may find themselves subject to exposure to transnational law enforcement without adequate legal protection is the transnational use of quasi-penal or civil measures such as freezing and forfeiture of assets without recourse to courts of law. The precarious position that the global terrorist asset freezing regime has placed individuals in well documented.[91] Early decisions of the General Court of the European Court of Justice found that these steps were not 'an arbitrary, inappropriate or disproportionate interference with the fundamental rights of the persons concerned'.[92] Eventually in the *Kadi*[93] decision in the Grand Chamber of the European Court of Justice clarified that the EU law transposing Security

---

88 See, for example, *Sianturi and others v Indonesia*, Constitutional Review, Nos 2, 3/PUU-V/2007; ILDC 1041 (ID 2007), 23 October 2007. See Rick Lines, 'A "Most Serious Crime"? The Death Penalty for Drug Offences and International Human Rights Law' (2010) 21 *Amicus Journal* 21.

89 Reprieve, *The Death Penalty and Drug Offences: UNODC and Donor State Responsibility* (2015), available at http://www.ohchr.org/Documents/HRBodies/HRCouncil/DrugProblem/Reprieve.pdf.

90 See, for example, UNODC, *Technical Programme on Drugs and Crime in the Islamic Republic of Iran 2011–2014* (Vienna, 2011), available at <https://www.unodc.org/documents/islamicrepublicofiran/CP_Iran11–14.pdf> last visited 8 November 2017. It includes a sub-programme on 'Illicit trafficking and Border Management' aimed at enhancing interdiction capacity and identifying organized crime networks as well as 'serious operatives'.

91 See, for example Jude McCulloch and Sharon Pickering, 'Suppressing the Financing of Terrorism: Proliferating State Crime, Eroding Censure and Extending Neo-Colonialism' in (2005) 45 *British Journal of Criminology* 470, 475.

92 *Kadi v Council and Commission* (2005), Case T-315/01, Para. 251.

93 Case C-402/05 P and C-415/05, *P. Kadi and Al Barakaat International Foundation v. Council and Commission* [2008] ECR I–6351.

Council Resolutions which provided for the freezing of the appellant's assets as a suspected member of Al Qaeda without reasons or opportunity to be heard, must give way to the human rights obligations that apply as the EU's fundamental law.[94] But even within the EU these sorts of limits on executive freedom of action are themselves limited in scope because courts are willing to grant the authorities a wide margin of appreciation before limits are imposed.

Despite the fact that a significant amount of effort has been put into the globalisation of criminal justice rights in the post-war period, the human rights regime is thus not yet fully in place in the transnational penal space. The global human rights regime has largely focussed on overarching top-down protections though instruments that try to project protections into the transnational penal space, not always that successfully, because transnational criminal law is imbued with concepts of sovereignty and severity that serve to block that projection. More obviously, states can pick and choose when it comes to the protection of rights both in the negotiation, acceptance and monitoring of transnational criminal laws. For example, in the mini-Brexit of 2013 the UK opted into the European Arrest Warrant (EAW) but only into two of the six directives to strengthen the procedural rights of suspected or accused persons in criminal proceedings promulgated by the EU to make up for fair trial shortcomings in the EAW directive.[95]

The weakness and fragmentation of a basic, globalised, transnational standard for a 'fair trial' beyond a state's domestic criminal jurisdiction, lies at the heart of these examples of uneven human rights treatment.[96] Gless makes the

94 See Juliane Kokott and Christoph Sobotta, 'The Kadi-Case—Constitutional Core Values and International Law Finding the Balance' 23 *European Journal of International Law* (2012) 1015.

95 See generally House of Lords European Union Select Committee, Ninth Report, The UK's opt-in Protocol: implications of the Government's approach, 10 March 2015, chapter 2. The relevant directives spawned by the EU's roadmap for strengthening procedural rights of suspected or accused persons in criminal proceedings include: Directive 2016/343 of 9 March 2016 on the strengthening of certain aspects of the presumption of innocence and of the right to be present at the trial in criminal proceedings; Directive 2012/29 of 25 October 2012 establishing minimum standards on the rights, support and protection of victims of crime; Directive 2011/0129 of 18 May 2011 establishing minimum standards on the rights, support and protection of victims of crime; Directive 2010/64 of 20 October 2010 on the right to interpretation and translation in criminal proceedings; Directive 2012/13 of 22 May 2012 on the right to information in criminal proceedings; and Directive 2004/80 of 29 April 2004 relating to compensation to crime victims.

96 Gless and Vervaele (n 24), 6.

point that when international instruments for the suppression of crime are developed, state participants seem primarily concerned with the establishment and enforcement of their own *ius puniendi* and the limitation of the *ius puniendi* of other states, rather than with the plight of the individuals subject to the system.[97] In a system where states retain their independent authority to enforce their jurisdiction, yet are urged to cooperate, defendants may find themselves subject to multiplications of penal power created by an incoherent patchwork of laws made up of overlapping national criminal jurisdictions.[98]

'Bad global citizens' subject to transnational criminal law in the 'transnational penal space' are not outlaws because they are not sovereign free, but nor are they full persons under the laws of the state seeking to extend its jurisdiction extraterritorially.[99] They are to be policed as others, not as a part of the self, by means of international cooperation. As Dubber puts it, this involves 'an a-legal conception of international law as inter-sovereign relations, a realm where householders meet for tea to coordinate the disposal of human nuisances.'[100] He argues that the state policing extraterritorially does not behave as a *Rechtstaat* but as a police State, because the exercise of its extraterritorial jurisdiction involve exercises in police cooperation and extradition, rules of international law, not criminal law.[101] In parallel to erosion of the autonomy of the state of refuge, the impact of transnational criminal law degrades the status of that person in their state of refuge. The 'transnational penal space' is therefore not a space devoid of law; it is filled with law, but potentially instrumental and unrestrained law. Walter Benjamin[102] argued that law of this kind is paradoxically always in danger of losing any vestige of legality and transforming into exercises of pure coercion. Benjamin called this 'mythic violence', a violence which produces 'bare life', the life of the people produced by this legal violence—culpable, naturally guilty.[103] At its worst, transnational criminal law can leave the 'bad global citizen', metaphorically 'naked', in the 'transnational penal space'.

---

97 Sabine Gless, 'Birds-Eye View and Worm's Eye View: Towards a Defendant-Based Approach in Transnational Criminal Law' 6(1) *Transnational Legal Theory* (2015) 117, 119 et seq.

98 Ibid., 127.

99 See Dubber (n 2), 249 et seq.

100 Ibid., 277.

101 Ibid., 261.

102 W. Benjamin, 'Towards a Critique of Violence' in *Selected Writings*, ed. Marcus Bollock; Michael W. Jennings, 4 vols. (Cambridge, Mass.: Belknap Press of Harvard UP, 1996), 242.

103 Ibid., 250.

IV 'Global Citizenship' for 'Bad Global Citizens'

May contends that only global citizenship will ensure global justice, in the sense that individuals have access to the rule of law and procedural fairness wherever they may be.[104] A step in constituting this citizenship would be, as Gless advocates, adoption of an approach that places the individual defendant at the centre of transnational criminal relations, not as an object, but as a rights holder. She argues that states seeking cooperation from other states against transnational criminals through extradition must provide a functional equivalent to the constitutional protections they afford their own citizens who are exposed to prosecution.[105] She supports, as a concrete measure, the adoption of a global rule against double jeopardy that does not only prevent double prosecution for the same actions, but also prevents parallel prosecution, and deals with situations where some states criminalise a particular activity while other states do not.

The globalisation by states of rights and protections to protect 'bad global citizens' during the process of the development and implementation of transnational criminal law is a necessary step to granting these bad citizens the quality of protection any citizen deserves, and to clothe them in the transnational penal space. These principles should meet general concerns about the legitimacy of state action in the 'transnational penal space' in the sense of transparency, rationality and accountability.[106] To this end transnational criminal law needs principles of criminalisation, as well as principles of establishment and enforcement of jurisdiction. Gless makes the point that these global principles have to shape and direct the application of national rules in these situations. She suggests that they can be deduced from the normative aims of transnational criminal law or through empirical analysis of existing rules within the system.[107] This would involve infusing substantive and procedural principles of criminal legality into Dubber's "tea party". To put it plainly: individuals should be entitled to notice of both the jurisdiction and the substance of criminal laws,[108] to due process, and to reasonable treatment. More generally, however,

---

104 Larry May, *Global Justice and Due Process* (Cambridge: CUP, 2011), 198 et seq.

105 Gless (n 96), 130–4.

106 See Benedict Kingsbury, Nico Krisch and Richard B. Stewart, (2005) 68 'The Emergence of Global Administrative Law' (2005) 68 *Law and Contemporary Problems* 15.

107 Gless (n 96), 136.

108 Teresa Scassa and Robert J. Currie, 'New First Principles? Assessing the Internet's Challenges to Jurisdiction' (2010–11) 42 *Georgetown Journal of International Law* 1017, 1079.

given the inequality of sovereign relations in the 'transnational penal space', the decision to criminalise itself should be taxed against a precautionary governing principle: a willingness to question criminalization and procedural co-operation as a response to certain practices.

There does appear to be a growing consciousness, if only at a rhetorical level, of the need to protect the rights of transnational criminals. Recently, for example, the UN General Assembly adopted a resolution[109] at the 2016 Special Session of the UN General Assembly on the world drug problem in which states agreed to

> (*o*) Promote and implement effective criminal justice responses to drug-related crimes to bring perpetrators to justice that ensure legal guarantees and due process safeguards pertaining to criminal justice proceedings, including practical measures to uphold the prohibition of arbitrary arrest and detention and of torture and other cruel, inhuman or degrading treatment or punishment and to eliminate impunity, in accordance with relevant and applicable international law and taking into account United Nations standards and norms on crime prevention and criminal justice, and ensure timely access to legal aid and the right to a fair trial.

This is a very positive first step, but it is only one set of mainly procedural and treatment recommendations in regard to the drug control regime. The problem is that transnational penal spaces are frequently the creation of multiple transactions relating to different crimes. It seems more sensible to try to harmonise State practice in these spaces through application of a set of principles that apply to all transnational crimes.[110]

Full realisation of human rights protection of global bad citizens requires a conscious scrutiny of steps to engage in effective crime control. A rough framework for criminal justice policymaking to govern the transnational penal space should ask inter alia, the following principle based questions about any proposed new international instrument for the suppression of crime (including soft law regulatory instruments):

---

109 GA Res S-30/1, 4 May 2016.

110 Mirelle Delmas-Marty, *Ordering Pluralism: A Conceptual Framework for Understanding the Transnational Legal World* trans by N. Norberg (Oxford and Portland: Hart, 2009), 14, 17 et seq.

General

a) What evidence supports the identification of specific threats as harmful and does it justify either the use of criminal sanction or the use of the specific procedural mechanisms recommended?
b) Will the proposed instrument be of some measurable benefit to all?
c) Are the significant provisions in the proposed treaty/international instrument etc. legally acceptable to all potential parties and not bound to any single legal tradition?[111]
d) Does the proposed instrument adhere to the principle of legality by vesting the jurisdiction to prescribe certain crimes and to adjudicate and enforce those crimes in a competent lawmaker?[112]
e) Does the proposed instrument adhere to *lex certa*, i.e. is what is to be criminal is readily known and available, certain and clear?[113]

Principles for substantive criminalisation and punishment

f) Does the proposed instrument embrace the principle of personal guilt as a prerequisite to criminal liability[114] by making clear provision for conduct and fault in the definitions of proposed criminal offences?[115]
g) Does the proposed instrument embrace the principles of certainty of punishment, i.e. by making clear provision for the type, measure, and imminence of punishment to be meted out?[116]

Principles for the establishment of criminal jurisdiction

h) Does the proposed instrument adopt clear and recognised principles of jurisdiction, both territorial and extra-territorial, which establishes a

111 Stefanie Bock, 'The Prerequisite of Personal Guilt and the Duty to Know the LAW in the Light of Article 32 ICC Statute' 9 *Utrecht Law Review* (2013) 184.

112 Michiel J.J.P. Luchtman, 'Towards a Transnational Application of the Legality Principle in the EU's Area of Freedom, Security and Justice?' 9 *Utrecht Law Review* (2013) 11, 13, 14.

113 Danielle Ireland-Piper, 'Prosecutions of Extraterritorial Conduct and the Abuse of Rights Doctrine' 9 *Utrecht Law Review* (2013) 68, 87.

114 Bock (n 110), 184.

115 Ibid.

116 Cesare Beccaria, *On Crime and Punishment*, Trans. Henry Paolucci (Englewood Cliffs, New Jersey: Prentice Hall, 1963), 55–58. He separated this out from the necessity of clarity of the substantive law—see 17.

sufficiently close connection between the State concerned and the alleged crime in question to justify that State establishing jurisdiction?

i) Does the instrument spell out clearly a theory of precedence in cases of concurrent jurisdiction?

Principles for the enforcement of criminal jurisdiction through procedural cooperation

j) Does the instrument prohibit double jeopardy (*ne bis in idem*) so as to avoid the prospect of repeat prosecution or parallel prosecution for essentially the same offending?
k) Does the proposed instrument guarantee respect for human rights such as privacy in exchange and storage of information whether pre-investigation, for the purposes of investigation, or for the purposes of trial?
l) Does the proposed instrument guarantee respect for human rights and fair treatment at all stages of proceedings from investigation through to punishment, including enjoyment of all rights and guarantees provided by the domestic law of the Party in the territory in which that person is present?
m) Does the proposed instrument provide that all criminal charges be brought before a tribunal established by law, or in the case of administrative action, include the right of the judiciary to exercise oversight?

Closing the 'transnational penal space' is impractical given the proliferation of cross-border crime. But these general principles, many derived from domestic criminal law and policy-making, may go some way towards re-clothing the 'bad global citizen' in the transnational penal space.

Conclusion: Why Bother with the 'Bad Global Citizen'?

Luchtman questions the basis for granting rights to bad global citizens under transnational criminal law, noting that it is not clear why we should bother.[117] In contrast, the motivation for the adoption of transnational criminal law itself is clear: effective suppression. Cotterrell notes that from a Weberian perspective the main problem of transnational criminalisation is whether there is adequate political authority to engage in this activity, while from a Durkheimian

117 Luchtman (n 111), 11.

perspective the issue is whether there is adequate cultural authority to do so.[118] Durkheimian solidarity[119] appears to be lacking because it does not appear on the whole that the development of transnational criminal law either emanates from or results in an organic solidarity between peoples in different states in support of the suppression of these crimes.[120] The creation and application of transnational criminal law (in what Dubber calls an exercise of 'heteronomous power' by one sovereign over another) appears to be the product of executive coordination of a kind that would be more familiar to Weber. If there is solidarity, it is limited to the solidarity of the technocrats who run the 'transnational penal space'; a mechanical solidarity of the kind that Somek suggests underpins the retributive instincts that animate criminal justice.[121] Mechanical solidarity will not provide fertile ground for the granting of rights to the 'bad global citizen'. Technocrats may structure a fictional legal space to suppress crime, but their priority is not the creation of transnational communities committed to better human rights protection for individuals. How to make it so?

Relying on the legitimation of state power by the individuals subject to that power themselves, using social contract theory Wade argues that the kinds of power transferred via transnational law are lent conditionally on their being bundled together with citizen's rights.[122] However, the examples discussed in this piece show that for pragmatic reasons states have been willing to apply only limited conditions on placing their law enforcement power at the disposal of other states in regard to foreigners and increasingly to their own citizens. We must have resort to normative arguments in support of greater restraint. Somek's concept of cosmopolitan self-determination suggests a universal justification of a neo-Kantian kind to secure the precarious position of the 'bad global citizen' in the 'transnational penal space'.[123] In his view, in today's cosmopolitan global world individuals who move from one political community to another have the right to expect the same standards of protection as locals

118 Roger Cotterrell, 'The Concept of Crime and Transnational Networks of Community' in Valsamis Mitsilegas, Peter Alldridge and Leonidas Cheliotis (eds), *Globalisation, Criminal Law and Criminal Justice* (London: Hart, 2015) 7, 10 et seq.

119 Emile Durkheim, *The Division of Labour in Society* (Tran. W. D. Hall, New York, Free Press, 1964).

120 See Martti Koskenniemi, *The Gentle Civilizer of Nations: The Rise and Fall of International Law 1870–1960* (Cambridge: CUP, 2002), 297–300.

121 Alexander Somek, 'From the Rule of Law to the Constitutionalist Makeover: Changing European Conceptions of Public International Law' (2011) 18(4) *Constellations* 567, 568.

122 Wade (n 54), 180, 181.

123 Alexander Somek, 'On Cosmopolitan Self-Determination' (2012) 1(3) *Global Constitutionalism* 405, 406 et seq.

because they are human.[124] The only condition is that the political communities involved—the states generating transnational penal spaces—must commit themselves to the notional detachment of the cosmopolitan citizen from all communities. Can transnational criminal law generate laws that do so and thus pass cosmopolitan muster? Or to put it another way, are the crimes and criminal procedures to which the 'bad global citizen' is subject in the transnational legal space rational enough to be willed by anyone in regard to any human being, or are they in some sense special derogations of normal standards because they regulate the 'bad global citizen' in the 'transnational penal space' who is somehow different from the rest of us?

Lest we need reminding, 'bad global citizens' are human too, and we can all potentially be such 'bad global citizens'. Ironically, the need to protect 'bad global citizens' is likely to become more pressing as individuals take advantage of the commercial opportunities presented by current global problems. The market potential is enormous, for example, for the trafficking in the victims of global warming and the smuggling of people attempting to escape drowning and burning lands. On current form, the most likely response from increasingly stretched governments is harsh process and treatment unless it is tempered by placing human rights at the centre of transnational criminal law.

---

124 Ibid., 411.

Treaty Monitoring and Compliance in the Field of Transnational Criminal Law

Cecily Rose
Grotius Centre for International Legal Studies, Leiden Law School, Leiden University, The Netherlands
c.e.rose@law.leidenuniv.nl

Abstract

Most transnational criminal law treaties do not benefit from any sort of monitoring mechanism that would allow states parties or other actors to assess their domestic implementation and enforcement. There are a few exceptions, as treaties and other instruments concerning drug control, corruption, and money laundering are indeed accompanied by monitoring mechanisms. But the general pattern across the field of transnational criminal law is clear. This article explores some possible explanations for why transnational criminal law treaties generally lack monitoring mechanisms, and it also highlights the significance of this absence from a compliance perspective. The article advocates not for the creation of more treaty monitoring bodies in the field of transnational criminal law, but instead seeks to explain their relative absence and its significance for the field. The argument, therefore, is not that monitoring bodies are necessarily desirable and ought to exist in greater numbers in this field, but rather that the absence of these bodies obscures information about compliance and impedes research about what these treaties are actually accomplishing. The current state of treaty monitoring in the field of transnational criminal law is significant because of the extent of what we do not know about the effects of these instruments.

Keywords

transnational criminal law – treaties – monitoring – compliance

 | DOI 10.1163/9789004365797_004

1 Introduction

The field of transnational criminal law has grown exponentially since the Second World War on account of extensive treaty making. Through the conclusion of treaty after treaty, states have agreed to criminalize certain conduct at the domestic level and to cooperate internationally. But the conclusion of these treaties has not, for the most part, been accompanied by efforts to monitor compliance with them after their entry into force. Most transnational criminal law treaties do not benefit from any sort of monitoring mechanism that would allow states parties or other actors to assess their domestic implementation and enforcement. There are a few exceptions: treaties and other instruments concerning drug control, corruption, and money laundering are indeed accompanied by monitoring mechanisms. But the general pattern across the field of transnational criminal law is clear, and the paucity of monitoring mechanisms in this field forms a notable contrast with other branches of public international law, such as human rights law and international environmental law. Treaties in these other fields of international law typically depend on treaty bodies to monitor implementation, gather data, and make recommendations for improving domestic implementation and even updating international norms.

This article posits some possible explanations for why transnational criminal law treaties generally lack monitoring mechanisms, and it also explores the significance of their absence from a compliance perspective. There are a number of possible explanations for this absence, which range in their methodological orientation. On a practical level, states may care to avoid the potentially burdensome and duplicative character of monitoring mechanisms. Another more legal explanation may lie in the very character of these treaties, which are inherently less forward-looking than, for example, international environmental law treaties and which do not depend on such bodies for their very operation. In addition, historical factors have also played a role. Like human rights treaties, drug control treaties benefit from monitoring mechanisms due in part to the historical legacy of institutions dating back to the League of Nations. On a sociological level, the sheer diversity and decentralized character of the transnational criminal law field may also contribute to this trend. Treaties concerning one form of criminal conduct are arguably unlikely to influence treaty-making efforts regarding other, unrelated forms of criminal behavior, given that the composition of delegations involved in treaty negotiations will often vary across the field. The field also lacks a true geographical or institutional center that might foster the spread of certain trends, such as treaty monitoring bodies. Finally, on a political level, this article does not discount the possibility that states have deliberately refrained from creating monitoring bodies due to a reluctance or disinterest in ensuring compliance with treaties that can have profound implications for domestic criminal justice systems.

This article advocates not for the creation of more treaty monitoring bodies in the field of transnational criminal law, but instead seeks to explain their relative absence and its significance for the field. Monitoring bodies in this field would allow for the collection and analysis of data about treaty implementation, and potentially also domestic enforcement. But without mechanisms to gather such information, states parties to transnational criminal law treaties cannot even begin to meaningfully assess compliance, let alone the effectiveness of these treaty-making efforts. The argument, therefore, is not that monitoring bodies are necessarily desirable and ought to exist in greater numbers in this field. The fact that treaty monitoring bodies can generate heavy reporting requirements for states is enough to make such an argument impractical. Rather, the article seeks to highlight how the absence of these bodies obscures information about compliance and impedes research about what these treaties are actually accomplishing. The current state of treaty monitoring in the field of transnational criminal law is significant because of the extent of what we do not know about the effects of these instruments.

The article begins by elaborating on the contrast between the transnational criminal law field and the field of human rights and environmental law with respect to the existence of monitoring mechanisms (Part II). The article then explores some explanations for this disparity (Part III) before concluding with some observations on how the absence of monitoring mechanisms affects or impedes assessments of the compliance and effectiveness of transnational criminal law treaties (Part IV).

II The Relative Paucity of Treaty Monitoring in the Transnational Criminal Law Field

Treaty making has been integral to the fields of human rights law and international environmental law, and treaties in these fields have, for the most part, established bodies responsible for monitoring implementation by states parties. In the field of transnational criminal law, by contrast, treaty bodies have been the exception rather than the rule. This section elaborates on the extent of the disparity between the fields of human rights law and environmental law, on the one hand, and the field of transnational criminal law, on the other.

This study covers universal treaties concluded after the Second World War, thus excluding regional treaties, as well as treaties concluded before and during the existence of the League of Nations. Treaty monitoring with respect to regional and universal treaties may not be comparable on account of the fact that treaties negotiated under the auspices of regional organizations, such as the Organization of American States, may lend themselves more readily to follow-up mechanisms within the framework of an existing regional entity. In addition, the challenges involved in monitoring a universal treaty with nearly 200 states parties are likely to be quite different than those involved in monitoring a regional treaty with a much smaller number of relatively like-minded states that are already members of the same regional organization. In comparing treaties from the same era, this study excludes transnational criminal law treaties from the pre-Charter era. These instruments, dating back as early as the 1840s, have few contemporaries in the fields of human rights law and environmental law, as treaty-making in these fields has been a predominantly post WWII phenomena.[1] Part III of this article does, however, trace the historical origins of some contemporary treaty bodies back to the League of Nations era, in an effort to explain why certain fields benefit from monitoring mechanisms while others do not. Finally, this study covers a wide range of major areas in the field of transnational criminal law, namely transnational organized crime; slavery, human trafficking and migrant smuggling; terrorism; drug trafficking; corruption; and money laundering.

A *Human Rights and Environmental Law Treaties*

Each of the nine core international human rights treaties currently benefits from a treaty body.[2] The 1966 International Covenant on Economic, Social and Cultural Rights was originally an outlier, as the Covenant itself does not provide

1 Treaty for the Suppression of the African Slave Trade, 20 December 1841, 2 Martens Nouveau Recueil Général des Traités 392.

2 International Convention on the Elimination of All Forms of Racial Discrimination (adopted 7 March 1966, entered into force 4 January 1969) 666 UNTS 212 (CERD); International Covenant on Civil and Political Rights (adopted 16 December 1966, entered into force 23 March 1976) 999 UNTS 171; International Covenant on Economic, Social and Cultural Rights (adopted 16 December 1966, entered into force 3 January 1976) 993 UNTS 3 (ICESCR); Convention on the Elimination of All Forms of Discrimination against Women (adopted 18 December 1979, entered into force 3 September 1981) 1249 UNTS 13; Convention against Torture and Other Cruel, Inhuman or Degrading Treatment or Punishment (adopted 10 December 1984, entered into force 26 June 1987) 1465 UNTS 112; Convention on the Rights of the Child (adopted 20 November 1989, entered into force 2 September 1990) 1577 UNTS 3; International Convention on the Protection of the Rights of All Migrant Workers and Members of Their Families (adopted 18 December 1990, entered into force 1 July 2003) 2220 UNTS 3; International Covenant for the Protection of All Persons from Enforced Disappearance (adopted 20 December 2006,

for a treaty body. In 1985, however, the Economic and Social Council rectified this by creating the Committee on Economic, Social and Cultural Rights.[3] The Committee on the Elimination of Racial Discrimination, established in 1969, is the precedent setter for all of the human rights treaty bodies, which take the same basic form. These bodies consist of independent experts who serve in their personal capacity, rather than as governmental representatives, and they meet twice a year, for three weeks at a time.[4] States must submit an initial report on domestic implementation efforts within a year after becoming parties, and then must report periodically, every 2–5 years.[5] On the basis of states' reports, the Committees issue 'concluding observations' in which they set forth their concerns and make recommendations to states parties.[6] Because there are now 9 different human rights treaty bodies, which monitor instruments that encompass some overlapping rights, the reporting demands for states that are parties to most or all of these treaties have become burdensome and somewhat duplicative.[7] In addition, the treaty bodies themselves have struggled to process reports in a timely manner due in part to resource constraints.[8]

Treaty monitoring bodies are also pervasive in the field of international environmental law, in which most treaties require some sort of reporting by states parties.[9] In fact, reporting is the only specific legal obligation imposed

entered into force 23 December 2010) A/RES/61/177; Convention on the Rights of Persons with Disabilities (adopted 13 December 2006, entered into force 3 May 2008) 2515 UNTS 3.

3 ECOSOC Res 1985/17; ICESCR art 16.

4 See e.g. CERD art 8.

5 Ibid. art 9.

6 Ibid.

7 John Morijn, 'Reforming United Nations Human Rights Treaty Monitoring Reform' (2011) 58 Netherlands International Law Review 295, 297.

8 James Crawford, 'The UN Human Rights Treaty System: A System in Crisis?' in Philip Alston and James Crawford (eds) *The Future of UN Human Rights Treaty Monitoring* (CUP 2000) 6–7.

9 Daniel Bodansky, 'The Role of Reporting in International Environmental Treaties' in Philip Alston and James Crawford (eds) *The Future of UN Human Rights Treaty Monitoring* (CUP 2000) 365. International Convention for the Regulation of Whaling (adopted 2 December 1946, entered into force 10 November 1948) 161 UNTS 72 (ICRW); Convention on the Prevention of Marine Pollution by Dumping of Wastes and Other Matter (adopted 29 December 1972, entered into force 30 August 1975) 1046 UNTS 138; Convention for the Protection of the World Cultural and Natural Heritage (adopted 16 November 1972, entered into force 17 December 1975) 1037 UNTS 151; Convention on International Trade in Endangered Species of Wild Fauna and Flora (adopted 3 March 1973, entered into force 1 July 1975) 993 UNTS 243 (CITES); Convention on the Prevention of Marine Pollution by Dumping of Wastes and Other Matter (adopted 29 December 1972, entered into force 30 August 1975) 1046 UNTS 138; Convention on Long-Range Transboundary Air Pollution (adopted 13 November 1979, entered into force

by some environmental law treaties.[10] The type of reporting required by environmental law treaties is somewhat more varied than in the human rights field. Like human rights treaties, some environmental treaties require states parties to report on domestic implementing legislation and regulations. The 1973 Convention on International Trade in Endangered Species (CITES), for instance, requires states parties to submit a biennial report on implementing legislation, regulations and administrative measures to the CITES Secretariat, which, among other things, makes recommendations on implementation.[11] But in contrast to human rights treaties, many environmental treaties also require states parties to submit a range of other information to monitoring bodies, including data on matters such as emissions,[12] permits granted for scientific research,[13] and waste dumped or incinerated at sea.[14] Taken together, monitoring bodies in the field of environmental law can play at least three different functions, namely evaluating implementation by states parties, promoting a process of internal policy reform, and establishing a factual basis for amending the normative requirements set out in these instruments.[15] Treaty monitoring in the environmental field has suffered from some of the same problems that have plagued human rights reporting, including a proliferation of reporting requirements as well as inaccurate, incomplete and late reports, and superficial reviews by treaty bodies.[16]

---

16 March 1983) 1302 UNTS 217; Protocol to the 1979 Convention on Long-Range Transboundary Air Pollution on the Reduction of Sulphur Emissions or their Transboundary Fluxes by at least 30 per cent (adopted 8 July 1985, entered into force 2 September 1987) 1480 UNTS 215; Vienna Convention for the Protection of the Ozone Layer (adopted 22 March 1985, entered into force 22 September 1988) 1513 UNTS 293; Montreal Protocol on Substances that Deplete the Ozone Layer (adopted 16 September 1987, entered into force 1 January 1989) 1522 UNTS 3; Basel Convention on the Control of Transboundary Movements of Hazardous Wastes and their Disposal (adopted 22 March 1989, entered into force 5 May 1992) 1673 UNTS 57; United Nations Framework Convention on Climate Change (adopted 9 May 1992, entered into force 21 March 1994) 1771 UNTS 107.

10 Bodansky (n 9), 365. See e.g. 1979 Convention on Long-Range Transboundary Air Pollution, art 9.

11 CITES arts VIII, XII.

12 1979 Convention on Long-Range Transboundary Air Pollution, arts 8, 10.

13 ICRW art VIII, Schedule para 30.

14 1972 Convention on the Prevention of Marine Pollution by Dumping of Wastes and Other Matter, art V.

15 Bodansky (n 9), 365–367.

16 Ibid. 361.

B *Transnational Criminal Law Treaties*

In the field of transnational criminal law, by contrast, monitoring mechanisms are a rarity. Most treaties make no provision for any type of monitoring body that would review reports on domestic implementation or other pertinent data. With the exception of drug trafficking treaties, the monitoring bodies that do exist are a relatively recent development.

1 Slave Trading, Human Trafficking, Migrant Smuggling, and Organized Crime

In concluding treaties on a range of related crimes—namely, slave trading, human trafficking, migrant smuggling, and organized crime—states have so far refrained from establishing any monitoring bodies. Treaties concluded in the 1950s concerning human trafficking, prostitution, and slavery simply require states parties to communicate implementing legislation and regulations to the UN Secretary-General.[17] But these treaties do not call on the UN Secretary-General, or any other body, to review these communications and to make recommendations on the basis of them. In addition, the 1957 Abolition of Forced Labour Convention, which states concluded under the auspices of the International Labour Organization (ILO), also does not require the ILO to monitor implementation, and, in fact, the treaty does not even require states parties to communicate their implementation efforts to the ILO.[18]

Two recent protocols concerning human trafficking and migrant smuggling have similarly refrained from establishing treaty bodies, although these protocols left the door open to this possibility, and negotiations on a review mechanism are ongoing. These two protocols, concluded in 2000, supplement the UN Convention against Transnational Organized Crime (UNCTOC), which provides that the Conference of Parties shall agree upon mechanisms for promoting and reviewing the implementation of the treaty.[19] But the Conference of Parties has yet to agree on a review mechanism, more than 16 years after the conclusion of the Convention and its protocols, and negotiations in recent years have not been particularly productive. Negotiations among states parties

17 Convention for the Suppression of the Traffic in Persons and of the Exploitation of the Prostitution of Others (adopted 21 March 1950, entered into force 25 July 1951) 96 UNTS 271, art 21; Supplementary Convention on the Abolition of Slavery, the Slave Trade, and Institutions and Practices Similar to Slavery (adopted 7 September 1956, entered into force 30 April 1957) 266 UNTS 3, art 8.

18 Abolition of Forced Labour Convention (International Labour Organisation Convention No. 105) (adopted 25 June 1957, entered into force 17 January 1959) 320 UNTS 291.

19 United Nations Convention on Transnational Organized Crime (adopted 15 November 2000, entered into force 29 September 2003) 2225 UNTS 209, art 32(3) (UNCTOC).

with respect to a review mechanism only began in 2009, and in the years since then, negotiators have failed to agree on basic issues such as what the structure and methodology of the review mechanism should be, and how it should be funded.[20] Negotiators might be expected to take the review mechanism for the UN Convention against Corruption (UNCAC) as a model, as UNCAC's monitoring mechanism was established relatively recently, in 2009, and the treaties are similar (indeed, UNCTOC led to the conclusion of UNCAC).[21] Yet, there appears to be resistance to burdening states parties to UNCTOC with yet more surveys and peer review processes. The United States, for instance, has argued that the creation of a 'costly, burdensome peer review process' for UNCTOC could 'divert resources and personnel away from the practical implementation of the Convention'.[22] Should the states parties to UNCTOC eventually agree on a review mechanism, it is likely to involve a less extensive, and less expensive monitoring system than UNCAC's.

2 Terrorism Suppression Conventions

The absence of review mechanisms in the field of transnational criminal law is arguably most notable with respect to the terrorism suppression conventions on account of the sheer number and range of treaties in this area. None of the 14 universal terrorism suppression conventions, concluded between 1963 and 2010, creates a monitoring body, even though these treaties were concluded under the auspices of existing international organizations that might have played such a role.[23] These conventions fall under the auspices not only

---

20 Conference of the Parties to the United Nations Convention against Transnational Organized Crime, 'Report of the Chair on the open-ended intergovernmental meeting to explore all options regarding an appropriate and effective review mechanism for the United Nations Convention against Transnational Organized Crime and the Protocols thereto held in Vienna from 28 to 30 September 2015', 14 October 2015, CTOC/COP/WG.8/2015/3, paras 16–41.

21 Meeting to explore all options regarding an appropriate and effective review mechanism for the United Nations Convention against Transnational Organized Crime and the Protocols thereto, 'Five Years of UNCAC Reviews—What have we learned?', 16 September 2015, CTOC/COP/WG.8/2015/CRP.3.

22 Conference of the Parties to the United Nations Convention against Transnational Organized Crime, 'Compilation of comments and views received from States on all options regarding an appropriate and effective review mechanism for the United Nations Convention against Transnational Organized Crime and the Protocols thereto', 5 August 2015, CTOC/COP/WG.8/2015/2, para 101.

23 Convention on Offences and Certain Other Acts Committed on Board Aircraft (adopted 14 September 1963, entered into force 4 December 1969) 704 UNTS 219; Convention for the Suppression of Unlawful Seizure of Aircraft (adopted 16 December 1970, entered into force 14 October 1971) 860 UNTS 105; Convention for the Suppression of Unlawful

of the United Nations, but also the International Civil Aviation Organization (ICAO), the International Atomic Energy Agency (IAEA), and the International Maritime Organization (IMO). In addition, Interpol plays a role with respect to the 1999 International Convention for the Suppression of the Financing of Terrorism, and the 1991 Convention on the Marking of Plastic Explosives for the Purpose of Detection established an International Explosives Technical Commission.

None of these organizations or entities is engaged in treaty monitoring. Instead, the conventions assign other, more limited roles to them (or no role at all). These bodies act mainly as repositories for information about terrorist incidents and as mechanisms for the exchange of information.[24] The International Explosives Technical Commission plays a somewhat more active role in evaluating technical developments and making recommendations for amendments to the technical annex to the 1991 Convention on the Marking

---

Acts against the Safety of Civil Aviation (adopted 23 September 1971, entered into force 26 January 1973) 974 UNTS 177; Convention on the Prevention and Punishment of Crimes against Internationally Protected Persons, including Diplomatic Agents (adopted 14 December 1973, entered into force 20 February 1977) 1035 UNTS 167; International Convention against the Taking of Hostages (adopted 17 December 1979, entered into force 3 June 1983) 1316 UNTS 205; Convention on the Physical Protection of Nuclear Material (adopted 3 March 1980, entered into force 8 February 1987) 1456 UNTS 124; Protocol for the Suppression of Unlawful Acts of Violence at Airports Serving International Civil Aviation (adopted 24 February 1988, entered into force 6 August 1989) 1589 UNTS 474; Convention for the Suppression of Unlawful Acts against the Safety of Maritime Navigation (adopted 10 March 1988, entered into force 1 March 1992) 1678 UNTS 201; Protocol to the Convention of 10 March 1988 for the Suppression of Unlawful Acts against the Safety of Fixed Platforms Located on the Continental Shelf (adopted 10 March 1988, entered into force 1 March 1992) 1678 UNTS 201; Convention on the Marking of Plastic Explosives for the Purpose of Detection (adopted 1 March 1991, entered into force 21 June 1998) 2122 UNTS 359; International Convention for the Suppression of Terrorist Bombings (adopted 15 December 1997, entered into force 23 May 2001) 2149 UNTS 256; International Convention for the Suppression of the Financing of Terrorism (adopted 9 December 1999, entered into force 10 April 2002) 2178 UNTS 197; International Convention for the Suppression of Acts of Nuclear Terrorism (adopted 13 April 2005, entered into force 7 July 2007) 2445 UNTS 89; Convention on the Suppression of Unlawful Acts Relating to International Civil Aviation (adopted 10 September 2010).

24 See e.g. 1970 Convention for the Suppression of Unlawful Seizure of Aircraft, art 11; 1988 Convention for the Suppression of Unlawful Acts against the Safety of Maritime Navigation, art 15.

of Plastic Explosives.[25] But the Commission does not monitor implementation of the Convention. Only the 1980 Convention on the Physical Protection of Nuclear Material, as amended in 2005, provides for a one-time review of implementation by the Conference of States Parties, as well as the possibility of future review conferences.[26] The amended Convention does not, however, go so far as to create a review body distinct from the Conference of States Parties, nor does it mandate periodic reviews.

Although the Terrorism Prevention Branch of the Vienna-based United Nations Office on Drugs and Crime (UNODC) plays a range of roles with respect to the terrorism suppression conventions, its responsibilities revolve around technical assistance and capacity building rather than treaty monitoring. The Terrorism Prevention Branch on UNODC supports states parties in drafting and reviewing domestic legislation that implements the terrorism suppression conventions, and it builds the capacity of domestic officials to implement these laws.[27] But the Terrorism Prevention Branch does so only at the request of states, and not as a part of a more formal, systematic effort to monitor implementation across states parties as a whole. Moreover, as a part of the UNODC, the Terrorism Prevention Branch has no formal link to these treaties—the treaties themselves make no reference to the Terrorism Prevention Branch, and the Branch operates independently from ICAO, IAEA, and IMO.

3 Drug Trafficking Conventions

The International Narcotics Control Board (Board or INCB), created by the 1961 Single Convention on Narcotic Drugs, represents the most significant and long-standing exception to the general rule that transnational criminal law treaties do not benefit from treaty monitoring bodies. All three of the drug trafficking treaties concluded post WWII carve out a substantial role for the Board as a body that provides technical assessments and also monitors domestic implementation.[28] The composition of the Board is somewhat different from

25 1991 Convention on the Marking of Plastic Explosives for the Purpose of Detection, arts V–VI.

26 1980 Convention on the Physical Protection of Nuclear Material, art 16.

27 UNODC, 'Terrorism Prevention, About Us', <https://www.unodc.org/unodc/en/terrorism/about-us.html>. Marta Requena, 'The Role of the United Nations Office on Drugs and Crime's Terrorism Prevention Branch' in Ben Saul (ed) *Research Handbook on International Law and Terrorism* (Edward Elgar 2014).

28 Single Convention on Narcotic Drugs (adopted 30 March 1961, entered into force 13 December 1964) 520 UNTS 151; Convention on Psychotropic Substances (adopted 21 February 1971, entered into force 1976) 1019 UNTS 175; United Nations Convention against

the human rights treaty bodies due to the inclusion of non-lawyer experts. The UN Economic and Social Council is responsible for electing the Board's 13 members, of whom 3 are technical experts with medical, pharmacological or pharmaceutical experience selected from a list of persons nominated by the World Health Organization.[29] The remaining 10 members are nominated by UN member states and serve in their independent capacity, much like the members of the human rights treaty bodies.[30]

The Board, which describes itself as a 'quasi-judicial body'[31] regularly reviews the adequacy of domestic drug control legislation and policies, as well as measures taken by states parties to combat drug trafficking and abuse, the functioning of domestic drug control administrations, and compliance with reporting obligations under the treaties.[32] The Board's review process includes a limited number of 'country missions' each year, which allow it to discuss drug control measures with domestic authorities and to obtain first-hand information about the drug control situation in the given state.[33] On the basis of these country missions and the information reported by states parties to it, the Board makes findings and confidential recommendations for remedial measures.[34]

The Board also plays a limited enforcement role with respect to the 1961 Single Convention on Narcotic Drugs and the 1971 Convention on Psychotropic Substances when the treaties' aims are 'being seriously endangered' by the failure of a state party to comply with its treaty obligations.[35] The Board may request consultations with the state party or request further explanations from it, and may then call upon the state party to adopt remedial measures, as considered necessary. This procedure remains confidential until the Board determines that the state party has failed to provide satisfactory explanations or adopt remedial measures. At this stage, the Board may call the matter to

Illicit Traffic in Narcotic Drugs and Psychotropic Substances (adopted 20 December 1988, entered into force 11 November 1990) 1582 UNTS 95.

29 1961 Single Convention on Narcotic Drugs, art 9(1)(a).

30 Ibid. art 9(1)(b).

31 International Narcotics Control Board, 'About', <https://www.incb.org/incb/en/about.html>.

32 International Narcotics Control Board, 'Treaty Compliance', <https://www.incb.org/incb/en/treaty-compliance/index.html>; International Narcotics Control Board, Report of the International Narcotics Control Board for 2015 (United Nations 2016), para 129.

33 International Narcotics Control Board, Report of the International Narcotics Control Board for 2015 (United Nations 2016), paras 156–161.

34 Ibid. para 160.

35 1961 Single Convention on Narcotic Drugs, art 14; 1971 Convention on Psychotropic Substances, art 19.

the attention of the states parties, ECOSOC, and the Commission on Narcotic Drugs (which assists ECOSOC in supervising the drug control treaties). The Board may also recommend that states parties stop importing and/or exporting drugs from the state concerned, and it may publish a report on the matter. The Board has apparently invoked these enforcement provisions with respect to a limited number of states parties, and has only pursued public, as opposed to confidential measures, in the case of Afghanistan concerning its widespread illicit poppy cultivation.[36]

4 Corruption and Money Laundering

The other notable exceptions to the general rule may be found in the anti-corruption and anti-money laundering fields, both of which emerged in the 1990s, much more recently than the field of drug control, which dates back to the 1912 Hague International Opium Convention. The 2003 UN Convention against Corruption, which followed close on the heels of UNCTOC and was inspired by it, required the Conference of the States Parties to establish, if necessary, 'any appropriate mechanism or body to assist in the effective implementation of the Convention'.[37] While negotiations concerning a review mechanism stretched on for several years, from 2006 to 2009, they were ultimately successful, and the Implementation Review Group (IRG) began operating in 2010. Since then, the IRG has carried out a relatively large-scale peer review process involving the treaty's nearly 180 states parties. On the basis of an extensive self-assessment checklist, a desk review, and a possible country visit, each state party is reviewed by two other states parties, which produce a country review report with the help of UNODC. This report, however, may only be published with the consent of the state party under review. The review process is phased, meaning that the IRG reviews the implementation of only a couple chapters of UNCAC in each review cycle. Given the length of UNCAC, which contains 71 articles, and its large number of states parties, the review process has unsurprisingly been delayed, and the first cycle is still ongoing as of this writing.

The most noteworthy monitoring of domestic implementation of anti-money laundering norms has taken place in connection with a non-binding instrument as opposed to a treaty. The 1988 UN Convention against Illicit Traffic in Narcotic Drugs and Psychotropic Substances was the first international

36 International Narcotics Control Board, 'Treaty Compliance', <https://www.incb.org/incb/en/treaty-compliance/index.html>; International Narcotics Control Board, Report of the International Narcotics Control Board for 2015 (United Nations 2016), paras 228–230.

37 United Nations Convention against Corruption (adopted 31 October 2003, entered into force 14 December 2005) 2349 UNTS 41 (UNCAC), art 63(7).

instrument to require the criminalization of money laundering, albeit in the specific context of drug trafficking. But the International Narcotics Control Board does not specifically concern itself with the implementation of the Convention's anti-money laundering provisions.[38] Instead, monitoring of anti-money laundering norms has taken place in relation to the 40 Recommendations of the Financial Action Task Force (FATF), which were first issued in 1990, and focus specifically on money laundering as well as terrorist financing. The FATF 40 Recommendations have benefited from a particularly robust, and at times arguably coercive review mechanism. Despite their non-binding status, the FATF 40 Recommendations have brought about domestic implementation of anti-money laundering provisions in much the same way as treaties like the 1988 UN Convention against Illicit Traffic in Narcotic Drugs and Psychotropic Substances and UNCTOC. The review mechanism attached to the 40 Recommendations may therefore be considered comparable to the other treaties discussed in this piece.

FAFT's review mechanism consists of 'mutual evaluations' or peer review among the organization's 37 members, which are substantially the same as the members of the Organisation for Economic Co-operation and Development (OECD). The review process involves country visits, and culminates in the publication of a mutual evaluation report. The first three rounds of mutual evaluations focused on implementation of the Recommendations, while the fourth round, which is currently ongoing, covers implementation as well as the effectiveness of members' anti-money laundering and counter-terrorist financing systems. When states fail to implement effective anti-money laundering and counter-terrorism financing systems, FATF's procedures also provide for enforcement through public peer pressure and even retorsion or 'countermeasures', as FATF calls them.[39] Unlike the other review mechanisms described in this study, FATF's review procedures and enforcement mechanisms extend to non-FATF members. In an effort to ensure world-wide implementation of anti-money laundering and counter-terrorist financing standards, FATF has developed a parallel evaluation procedure for assessing implementation of the Recommendations by non-members through what it terms 'FATF-Style Regional Bodies'. In addition, FATF's enforcement mechanisms have focused almost exclusively on non-FATF members.

38 1988 UN Convention against Illicit Traffic in Narcotic Drugs and Psychotropic Substances, art 3(b), (c).

39 FATF 40 Recommendations, Recommendation 19.

III Possible Explanations for the Relative Absence of Treaty Monitoring in the Field of Transnational Criminal Law

While treaty monitoring bodies are not entirely absent from the field of transnational criminal law, they are relatively scarce, in contrast with other fields of public international law, such as human rights and environmental law. This contrast begs for some explanations of what accounts for this disparity. Why do most transnational criminal law treaties lack accompanying monitoring mechanisms, which have become standard in other international legal fields?

A *Burdensome and Duplicative Reporting Requirements*

One of the most obvious explanations may be that states negotiating transnational criminal law treaties have been keen to avoid the burdensome and sometimes duplicative reporting requirements that monitoring mechanisms tend to generate. If all or even just many of the treaties in the field of transnational criminal law were associated with monitoring mechanisms that imposed regular reporting requirements on states parties, the demands on states would be considerable, if not overwhelming, given the sheer number of treaties in this field. The recent negotiations regarding the creation of a monitoring mechanism for UNCTOC show that states parties are indeed aware of the potential for burdensome requirements and are hesitant to impose more intensive reporting requirements on themselves. UNCAC's monitoring mechanism thus appears to have substantially diminished enthusiasm for the creation of other similar treaty bodies.

States' experiences with reporting requirements in the fields of human rights and environmental law may have also dampened enthusiasm for the creation of monitoring mechanisms in the field of transnational criminal law. But this can be no more than a partial explanation for the absence of monitoring bodies due to the fact that a number of transnational criminal law treaties predate the conclusion of human rights and environmental law treaties in the 1960s and 1970s. Moreover, reporting fatigue does not explain why states have, in the first place, generally been willing to take on burdensome reporting obligations with respect to human rights and the environment, but not transnational crime.

States could also conceivably view such mechanisms as duplicative in light of the role of that the United States has adopted in monitoring domestic responses to transnational crimes such as human trafficking. With its country-by-country approach, the annual 'Trafficking in Persons Report' produced by the US State Department resembles the type of report that might be produced by a treaty body engaged in monitoring and evaluating domestic implementation and enforcement of the Protocol to Prevent, Suppress and Punish Trafficking in Persons. But these reports are based not on reporting by states parties, but on information gathered by the State Department, which does not enjoy the sort of independent status that a treaty body would. In addition, the reports' treatment of the relevant international legal instrument is also fairly superficial by comparison to what a treaty body would be expected to produce.[40] Thus, the role played by the United States in monitoring domestic responses to human trafficking is also not a particularly persuasive explanation for states' reluctance to create a distinct treaty monitoring body.

B Character of the Treaties as Prospective or Reactive

A second possible explanation relates to the character of the treaties themselves. Treaties in the field of transnational criminal law could arguably be characterized as less forward looking or prospective than treaties in other fields, such as environmental law. Environmental law treaties often require the collection of data so that accompanying schedules or annexes can be updated periodically after the conclusion of the treaty. These treaties are also geared towards mitigating an ongoing problem with a view towards achieving or maintaining a particular result in the future. In order for these treaties to function properly, states parties often require information about the current state of implementation, as well as the ability to adjust the rules accordingly. Viewed from this perspective, monitoring bodies enable the operation of environmental law treaties.

Transnational criminal law treaties are arguably more retrospective, and do not obviously require treaty bodies capable of monitoring implementation. With the notable exception of drug trafficking treaties, transnational criminal law treaties mainly require the criminalization of a given set of conduct in response to ongoing problems or incidents in the relatively recent past. The terrorism suppression conventions illustrate this point, as states have adopted what is known as a 'sectoral approach' to treaty-making, whereby the negotiation of a treaty responds or reacts to a recent terrorism crisis or string of incidents.[41] The drafters of these treaties appear to have assumed that the agreed upon criminalization provisions represent appropriate solutions to the given conduct, and will not require periodic updating. Future updates are, at least, not contemplated by these treaties, unlike environmental law treaties.

---

40 US State Department, 2016 Trafficking in Persons Report, 36.

41 Kimberly N. Trapp, 'The Potentialities and Limitations of Reactive Law Making: A Case Study in International Terrorism Suppression' (2016) 39 *University of New South Wales Law Journal* 1191.

As a result, the drafters of terrorism suppression conventions may not have perceived a need to create a treaty body to which states could report both data and domestic implementation measures. The negotiation of terrorism treaties has thus been driven not by the collection of data or information about implementation, but by the ever-evolving methods of terrorists.

The drug trafficking treaties are an important exception to this characterization of transnational criminal law treaties as more retrospective than prospective, as their continued operation depends on the INCB's collection and analysis of information not only about domestic implementation, but also data on international trade in drug trafficking and required medical usage of certain substances. It must also be acknowledged that transnational criminal law treaties cannot be regarded as entirely retrospective, as criminalization provisions are geared not only towards retribution but also future deterrence and prevention. An entire chapter of UNCAC is, in fact, devoted to provisions concerning the prevention of corrupt conduct.[42]

C *Historical Origins of Monitoring Bodies*

A third possible explanation for the existence of certain monitoring bodies, or the lack thereof, may be found in the historical origins of some of the treaties examined in Part II. Treaty bodies in the fields of drug trafficking and human rights, for instance, have links to monitoring bodies that existed during the time of the League of Nations. In the drug trafficking field, monitoring bodies created in the 1920s and 30s have persisted over time, even as one treaty regime has been replaced by another. The existence of the INCB, for instance, may be explained partly by virtue of the fact that it represents the continuation of the Permanent Central Narcotics Board, which was created by the 1925 International Opium Convention and which began operating in 1929. The 1961 Single Convention on Narcotic Drugs ultimately terminated the 1925 International Opium Convention, as well as other drug trafficking treaties,[43] but it also provided for the INCB's adoption of the functions of the Permanent Central Board, and those of the Drug Supervisory Body, which was created by the 1931 Convention for Limiting Manufacture and Regulating Distribution of Narcotic Drugs.[44]

---

42 UNCAC chapter II.

43 International Opium Convention (adopted 19 February 1925, entered into force 25 September 1928) 81 LNTS 319, arts 19, 44.

44 1961 Single Convention on Narcotic Drugs, art 45; Convention for Limiting the Manufacture and Regulating the Distribution of Narcotic Drugs (adopted 13 July 1931, entered into force 1933) 139 LNTS 303, art 5(6). See generally I. Bayer and H. Ghodse, Evolution of

Some of the features of the current INCB are the legacy of inter-war politics and ideals, in particular its semi-independent status and its inclusion of expert members. In negotiating the 1925 International Opium Convention, the drafters' envisioned a central supervisory organ that reflected 'the inclinations of the period's internationalists and American progressives, who favoured expert committees, independent evaluators, and disinterested quasi-judicial bodies'.[45] The Permanent Central Board enjoyed semi-independence from the League of Nations, as it had 'full technical independence' from the Council of the League of Nations. The Secretary-General of the League of Nations did, however, exercise control over staff in administrative matters, and the Council was responsible for appointing members of the Board.[46] The 1925 International Opium Convention also required the Council to invite two non-members of the League, the United States and Germany, to nominate one person each to participate in these appointments.[47] In addition, the treaty ensured that the members of the Board included subject experts, namely persons with 'technical competence' and 'knowledge of the drug situation'.[48]

These provisions on the status and membership of the Permanent Central Board reflect political tensions during the inter-war period. The United States, which remained outside of the League of Nations, participated in these treaty negotiations but had an interest in avoiding direct cooperation with the League or bodies squarely within its organizational structure. Treaty negotiations thus culminated in a Permanent Central Board with semi-independence from the League, and members from two non-members of the League, the United States and Germany. With the conclusion of the 1961 Convention, these design features carried over to the INCB, which describes itself as an 'independent, quasi-judicial body' and includes expert members with medical, pharmacological or pharmaceutical experience. Semi-independent might, however, be a more apt description of the INCB, as the United Nations bears the expenses of the INCB, and ECOSOC is responsible for electing its members.[49]

In the human rights field, the existing treaty bodies represent not the continuation of pre WWII monitoring bodies, but the legacy of the League's

International Drug Control, 1945–1995 (1999) Bulletin on Narcotics; UNODC, A Century of International Drug Control (2008).

45 William McAllister, *Drug Diplomacy in the Twentieth Century: An International History* (2000) 60.

46 1925 International Opium Convention, art 20.

47 Ibid. art 19.

48 Ibid. art 19.

49 1961 Single Convention on Narcotic Drugs, arts 6, 9.

mandate system, which may be considered one of the precursors to the modern human rights system. Obvious differences between the mandates system and the present body of human rights law must, of course, be acknowledged. While the mandates system concerned only the 'well-being and development' of peoples in certain colonies and territories, human rights law is universal in its application. Yet the reporting system developed for the mandates system may be considered the precursor to the reporting systems developed in the UN era with respect to the Universal Declaration of Human Rights and the subsequent human rights treaties.

The Covenant of the League of Nations required all mandatory powers with territories committed to their charge to submit annual reports to the Council of the League.[50] The Covenant also established a Permanent Mandates Commission (PMC) responsible for receiving and examining these annual reports and advising the Council of the League on 'matters relating to the observance of the mandates'.[51] The PMC was composed of nine influential colonial experts who served in their personal capacity and met several times a year to consider reports by the mandatory powers.[52] The PMC viewed itself as a technical body responsible for ensuring that the mandatory powers adhered to the Covenant and their mandate agreements.[53] The PMC had an information-gathering function which it pursued through questionnaires that it designed for the mandatory powers.[54] These questionnaires eventually covered not only the mandatories' obligations as set out in the Covenant and the mandatory agreements, but also more extensive information about the political, administrative, economic, and social conditions in the territories.[55]

While the UN Trusteeship system is the direct successor to the League's mandate system, the PMC's influence can also be detected in the modern human rights system, which relies on reporting by states parties as the basis for treaty monitoring.[56] In 1956 ECOSOC began requiring UN members to report every three years on developments and progress achieved with respect to the rights set out in the Universal Declaration of Human Rights and the right

50 Covenant of the League of Nations, art 22(7).
51 Covenant of the League of Nations, art 22(9).
52 Ruth Gordon, 'Mandates', Max Planck Encyclopedia of Public International Law, last updated February 2013, paras 33, 36.
53 Ibid. para 33.
54 Ibid. para 35.
55 Ibid.
56 Ibid. 56.

of peoples to self-determination.[57] In the mid-1960s, with the conclusion of the 1965 Convention for the Elimination of All Forms of Racial Discrimination and the two 1966 Covenants, this reporting system developed into a key feature of the contemporary human rights system. Thus, while the progression from the Permanent Mandates Commission to human rights treaty bodies is not linear, the reporting mechanism developed by the PMC arguably left a legacy that continues to this day.

The existence of a review mechanism for UNCAC may also be explained, in part, by reference to a predecessor, if not a historical legacy going back to the League of Nations. The history of law-making in the anti-corruption field is far shorter than in the fields of drug trafficking and human rights, as it goes back no further than the 1990s, when the subject of corruption began to lose its taboo at international organizations. UNCAC's review mechanism cannot be described as having 'historical origins' in the OECD's Working Group on Bribery, the monitoring mechanism that accompanies the OECD Convention on Combating Bribery of Foreign Public Officials in International Business Transactions (OECD Anti-Bribery Convention).[58] But a clear influence may be traced. The mechanism developed by the OECD to monitor implementation of the OECD Anti-Bribery Convention in the late 1990s significantly influenced the creation of UNCAC's review mechanism in the mid to late 2000s. Following the conclusion of the OECD Anti-Bribery Convention in 1997, the parties to this treaty developed a robust peer review monitoring system in the form of the Working Group on Bribery. This body has carried out three different phases of review, which have concerned the implementation of the treaty, and the application and enforcement of domestic legislation. On the basis of questionnaires, desk reviews, and on-site visits, two reviewing states and the OECD Secretariat draft a report which makes recommendations for improved compliance by the state under review. The Working Group then adopts these reports and makes them publicly available.

The Working Group's use of peer review as the cornerstone of its review process is highly unusual among treaty bodies, but it is standard operating procedure for the OECD as an institution.[59] As this piece has shown, treaty bodies (with the exception of UNCAC's and FATF's review mechanisms) rely on assessments by expert bodies rather than peer states. In fact, before UNCAC,

57 ECOSOC Res 624B (XXII), para. 1.

58 Convention on Combating Bribery of Foreign Public Officials in International Business Transactions (adopted 17 December 1997, entered into force 15 February 1999) 37 ILM 1.

59 Fabrizio Pagani, 'Peer Review: A Tool for Co-operation and Change: An Analysis of an OECD Working Method', SG/LEG(2002)1 (2002).

peer review had never been used in connection with a treaty drafted under the auspices of the United Nations.[60] Given the related subject matter of the OECD Anti-Bribery Convention and UNCAC, the Conference of States Parties to UNCAC naturally looked to the relatively successful example set by the OECD Working Group on Bribery. Moreover, the expert members of many delegations from developed states were familiar with the peer review model of the OECD as well as FATF and the Council of Europe.[61] While states in favor of a peer review mechanism for UNCAC initially met with opposition, their position eventually prevailed after a number of developing states, which familiar with peer review in the context of FATF and the 1996 Inter-American Convention against Corruption, came to support its use in the context of UNCAC.[62] But the use of peer review among nearly 180 states parties to UNCAC has, unsurprisingly, proven more cumbersome than among the 41 relatively homogenous states parties to the OECD Anti-Bribery Convention. The reluctance of UNCTOC's Conference of Parties to adopt a similar review mechanism, due in part to concerns about overburdening states parties, suggests that the influence of the OECD Working Group on Bribery may have reached its limits.

D *The Highly Diverse Character of the Transnational Criminal Law Field*

A fourth possible explanation for the contrast sketched in Part II may be found in the highly diverse character of the field of transnational criminal law. The field encompasses a remarkably wide range of subjects, from slavery, drug trafficking, and terrorism, to corruption and money laundering. This forms a contrast with the human rights field, for example, in which all treaties concern rights that individuals hold in relation to the state, and there is even some overlap among these treaties. The environmental law field is more varied, with treaties that govern whaling, international trade in endangered species, marine and air pollution, the ozone layer, hazardous wastes, and climate change. Yet, all of these treaties focus on the protection of the environment, broadly defined.

The highly diverse character of the transnational criminal law field is arguably significant because it reduces the likelihood that one treaty will influence other law-making efforts, as diplomats or experts are unlikely to be involved in negotiating treaties across this rather broad field. A given negotiator might,

60 Matti Joutsen and Adam Graycar, 'When Experts and Diplomats Agree: Negotiating Peer Review of the UN Convention Against Corruption' (2012) 18 Global Governance 425, 426.

61 Ibid. 329–430.

62 Ibid. 432.

for instance, have in-depth, substantive knowledge of only one or a few related areas of the larger field of transnational criminal law. Transnational criminal law treaties admittedly have not been developed in complete isolation from each other, and they share a number of similar or identical features, such as provisions on extradition and mutual legal assistance. But the exceptionally broad range of subject matters in this field decreases the chances that governments would send the same individuals to negotiations for treaties concerning, for example, drug trafficking, terrorism, organized crime, and corruption. This, in turn, reduces the possibility that developments in one area of transnational criminal law will influence law-making in another area. The development of a monitoring mechanism for UNCAC played a role in triggering negotiations for a review mechanism for UNCTOC, a related treaty, but UNCAC's influence is unlikely to be more widespread. Even if the same ministry official were involved in a wide range of treaty negotiations, from drug trafficking to corruption, he or she could very well lack a high level of familiarity with the workings of treaty monitoring bodies in this field. As the negotiations for UNCAC demonstrate, the familiarity of negotiators with other review mechanisms can have a significant impact on the negotiation of other monitoring bodies. The breadth and diversity of the transnational criminal law field does not eliminate the possibility of such cross fertilization, but it does reduce the likelihood that treaties in one area will significantly influence law-making efforts in another.

Finally, transnational criminal law treaties arguably lack a single geographical or institutional base that might facilitate the spread of innovations between different areas of the field. The UN Office on Drugs and Crime was a relatively late entrant into the UN system, and is not in a strong position to mitigate the somewhat fragmented character of the field. UNODC was only established in 1997 through a merger of the UN Drug Control Programme and the Centre for International Crime Prevention.[63] Thus, during the first fifty years of post-WWII treaty making in the broad field of transnational criminal law (as opposed to the narrower area of drug control), states lacked a clear focal point for their activities in the form of the UNODC. During this period, states concluded treaties not only under the auspices of the United Nations, but also the ILO, IMO, IAEA, and ICAO. Even after the creation of UNODC in 1997, the transnational criminal law field has still lacked a clear center due to the continuing roles played by all of these institutions. By contrast, all of the human rights treaty bodies are supported by the Treaties Division of the Office of the High Commissioner for Human Rights, and they all meet in the same place, Geneva. This degree of

---

63 UNODC, 'About UNODC' <https://www.unodc.org/unodc/about-unodc/index.html?ref=menutop>.

centralization has arguably facilitated the development of a string of monitoring mechanisms with similar or identical working methods. The UNODC has not, and does not play the same role in the transnational criminal law field, which historically lacked a centralizing institution that could have fostered the development and coordination of treaty monitoring bodies.

E *Deliberate Omission*

A final, more speculative explanation could be that the relative absence of monitoring mechanisms in relation to transnational criminal law treaties reflects a deliberate choice on the part of negotiating states. States' participation in treaty negotiations may not always represent 'an authentic desire to suppress the particular conduct', but may instead reflect other considerations, such as pressure from other states, the promise of aid, or reputational concerns.[64] Thus, in drafting treaties in this field, states may have opted not to create monitoring bodies that could supervise domestic implementation and enforcement because they had little or no interest in holding themselves accountable in this manner. The negotiation and conclusion of transnational criminal law treaties may not, in other words, be matched by a real interest, among at least some states parties, in rigorous implementation and in having their compliance monitored. This is not to argue that states necessarily act in bad faith in entering into these treaties, but that states may participate in negotiations on account of political rather than legal considerations. Some states may have little enthusiasm for the project in the first place, and are therefore unlikely to pursue the creation of monitoring bodies.

This disinterest or resistance may also reflect the fact that treaties in this field concern matters that go to the core of domestic criminal justice systems. They involve sensitive decisions about what we deem to be criminal behavior worthy of punishment, and about how to allocate the time and resources of police, prosecutors, and judges. Transnational criminal law treaties arguably require states to alter core aspects of their public order, in ways that environmental law treaties, for example, do not. These treaties may also requires states to alter or abandon long-standing procedural or substantive rules of criminal law.[65] States' reluctance to embrace the transnational regulation of criminal law has manifested itself in the inclusion of a provision on the protection of sovereignty in a number of transnational criminal law treaties (whereby states commit to carry out their treaty obligations in a manner consistent with

64 Neil Boister, *An Introduction to Transnational Criminal Law* (OUP 2012) 262.

65 Ibid. 20.

'sovereign equality' and 'non-interference').[66] In restating these fundamental rules of public international law, states appear to be signaling some resistance to the project at hand.

Given the implications that these treaties can have for domestic legal systems, it is perhaps unsurprising that states have at times entered into some or many transnational criminal law treaties with a degree of trepidation or reluctance. In some cases, omission of monitoring mechanisms could therefore represent a purposeful, strategic decision to avoid any sort of supervision of domestic implementation and enforcement. States may, in other words, have an interest in keeping the lid on whatever gap exists between what states have committed to on paper, and what they do in practice.

IV Some Concluding Observations on the Implications of Sparse Monitoring of Transnational Criminal Law Treaties

The relative absence of monitoring mechanisms in the transnational criminal law field has some significant implications for our capacity to assess the functioning of these treaties. Without comprehensive, cross-national data about implementation as well as enforcement of treaty obligations in this field, it is very difficult to meaningfully analyze compliance by states with their treaty obligations, as well as the effectiveness of these instruments. The argument is not that there ought to be more monitoring bodies. There are admittedly many reasons not to establish such bodies. They can impose burdensome reporting requirements on states ill-equipped to meet these demands, and they are costly, especially when country-visits are involved. This piece also does not advocate for monitoring bodies as necessarily beneficial mechanisms, though there are many potential benefits. Monitoring bodies can facilitate legislative reform and the exchange of best practices and they can also form the basis for updating the treaty itself. Instead, this section reflects on the broader consequences of failing to monitor, and what this means for the integrity of the field as a whole.

The fields of international law and international relations together boast an array of theories about why states do or do not comply with their international legal obligations. These theories identify various reasons for compliance, including national interest, the inherent fairness or legitimacy of the rules themselves, reputational concerns, and the internalization of international rules in

66 Ibid. See e.g. 1988 UN Convention against Illicit Traffic in Narcotic Drugs and Psychotropic Substances, art 2; UNCTOC art 4; UNCAC art 4.

domestic legal systems.[67] All of these theories, however, assume the existence of information about compliance—information which tends to be anecdotal rather than empirical. In the transnational criminal law field, however, this assumption about the existence of information may not be valid on account of the relative absence of monitoring bodies that might collect and make such information available. When considered from the perspective of these compliance theories, the relative absence of monitoring mechanisms in the transnational criminal law field reveals a troubling inability to discuss matters of compliance in an accurate and meaningful manner. Reporting by states about implementation and enforcement greatly facilitates assessments of compliance, which would otherwise be difficult if not impossible due to a lack of publicly available information.

At the same time that the field of transnational criminal law does not, for the most part, allow for the application of these compliance theories, the field itself also reveals a weakness in the existing theories, which are generally premised on anecdotal as opposed to empirical information. The existing theories generally concern specific instances of compliance or non-compliance, often in the area of peace and security.[68] In the transnational criminal law field, however, anecdotal information about treaty implementation and enforcement forms an unsatisfactory basis for assessing compliance, and the same may be true in other areas, including peace and security. Meaningful assessments of compliance by states with particular treaty obligations require cross-national information over a substantial period of time. Anecdotal information about non-compliance by one or two states may be exceptional or representative—it is difficult to make this determination without more empirical information.

On account of the challenges involved in acquiring and analyzing cross-national data, international legal fields that are dominated by treaties that require domestic implementation and enforcement may push the limits of these compliance theories. The need to obtain cross-national data in the certain fields, and the problems involved in doing so have not been a focus of compliance theories. These theories have arguably devoted too little attention to this methodological problem, which calls for more consideration of what questions we

---

67 See e.g. A. Chayes and A.H. Chayes, *The New Sovereignty: Compliance with International Regulatory Agreements* (Harvard University Press 1995); Thomas Franck, *Fairness in International Law and Institutions* (Clarendon 1995); A. Guzman, A Compliance-Based Theory of International Law' (2002) 90 *California Law Review* 1823; Harold Koh, 'Why Do Nations Obey International Law' (1997) 106 *Yale Law Journal* 2599.

68 Andrew T. Guzman, 'A Compliance-Based Theory of International Law' (2002) *California Law Review* 1823, 1885.

currently cannot answer because of gaps in available data, why we lack certain information, and how we might resolve these gaps in information.

Without empirical studies of compliance, assessments of the effectiveness of transnational criminal law treaties are difficult, if not impossible. The existence of information about treaty compliance is a necessary first step towards being able to assess whether transnational criminal law treaties are effectively preventing or reducing a particular form of conduct, facilitating international cooperation, etc. In order to make assessments about whether the criminalization of various forms of terrorism, for instance, represents an effective way of combating this phenomenon, it is necessary to establish, as a preliminary matter, whether states have actually enacted and enforced implementing legislation. The experience of FATF demonstrates that even with a great deal of information about compliance, assessing effectiveness is a highly complex endeavor that may require years of further peer reviews. The assessments of effectiveness currently being undertaken by FATF as well as the OECD Working Group on Bribery are, of course, very much the exception in the field of transnational criminal law.

The fact that international organizations and researchers generally lack the capacity to assess the compliance and hence the effectiveness of most transnational criminal law treaties creates a high level of uncertainty about the existing treaty regimes in this field. States have developed a relatively vast body of treaty law that may or may not be adequately designed to combat transnational crimes. The field of transnational criminal law is unusual in that most of the treaties make no provision for follow-up to ensure that domestic implementation and enforcement is not only proceeding as desired, but also having the expected effect. The result is a remarkable gap between the extensive law-making undertaken by states with respect to transnational crimes, and our capacity to establish what this actually accomplishes.

Transnational Organization, Transnational Law and the Ambiguity of Interpol in a World Ruled with Law

James Sheptycki
York University in Toronto, Canada
jshep@yorku.ca

Abstract

Using the practical empirical example of the Interpol Organization, the paper explores the relationship between transnational organization and transnational law. *Pace* Jessup's pioneering work in 1956, the central questions surrounding the notion of transnational law have involved understanding the use of legal tools in an administrative grey area of global governance across a range of legal institutions. This essay demonstrates how Interpol constituted as itself a formal 'Intergovernmental Organization' with its own self-governing structure and explores the use of one of its most powerful legal tools: the Red Notice. As a formally constituted IGO with transnational reach and legally subject to its own constituted governance processes, Interpol is an example of what Neil Walker calls 'constitutionalism beyond the State'. *A fortiori*, Interpol mobilizes a range of legal tools from transnational public international law and criminal law, as well as those of its own constitutional order, in making up its organization. Following Terence C. Halliday and Gregory Shaffer, and based on this empirical case study, the essay argues that Interpol is an important constituent element in the broader 'transnational legal order' of global policing. The challenge for socio-legal scholarship is to reveal how the transnational legal order of which Interpol is a part, is shaped by a variety of actors using different kinds of legal instruments because the institutional patterns thereby established have consequences for future developments. The transnational legal order of global policing is a synecdoche of global governance more generally and the specific case of Interpol provides the basis of some general claims about how to understand the concept of law under transnational conditions. The essay argues that Interpol is but a small constituent element of an evolving global system of rule *with* law. Rule with law emphasizes that in all practical circumstances legal tools are in the hands of knowing social actors. Understood this way, law is practical politics undertaken by means of legal tools. Interpol is but one element of a vast transnational legal order that has no democratic basis and which needs to be progressively uncovered through piecemeal empirical case studies. Read against the backdrop of broad

 | DOI 10.1163/9789004365797_005

socio-legal theory, such case studies offer critical insights concerning contemporary transnational legal ordering.

Keywords

interpol – transnational organization – transnational law – transnational legal order – transnational criminal law – constitutionalism beyond the state

Introduction

Interpol is a much mythologized and little understood institution. This paper uses an examination of this global police organization to explore the theoretical notions of 'transnational organization' and 'transnational law' using the empirical example of Interpol to illustrate the relationship between them in the formation of a transnational legal order. It explores both the legal constitution of Interpol and one of its most potent legal tools—the Interpol Red Notice. Interpol Red Notices are often thought of as the equivalent of an international arrest warrant but are really little more than world-wide wanted posters. For some the Interpol Red Notice is a quasi-legal instrument with transnational reach which has to be taken seriously because Interpol has successfully constituted itself into a transnational legal order. Halliday and Shaffer define a transnational legal order as a "collection of formalized legal norms and associated organizations and actors that authoritatively order the understanding and practice of law across national jurisdictions".[1] Interpol is a key constituent in the transnational legal order of global policing.[2] The empirical example of Interpol offers a litmus test concerning an emerging transnational legal, social, professional and political space and gives specificity to the theoretical notion of a transnational legal order. The most general feature of this legal order is that it is ruled *with* law.[3]

---

1 Halliday, Terence C. and Shaffer, Gregory (eds) (2015) *Transnational Legal Orders*, Cambridge: Cambridge University Press, p. 7.

2 Bowling, B. and Sheptycki, J. (2012) *Global Policing*, London: Sage.

3 Bowling, B. and Sheptycki, J. (2015) 'Global Policing and Transnational Rule with Law' in *Transnational Legal Theory*, Vol. 6 No. 1, pp. 141–173.

By 'transnational organization' is meant a structure that enables transactions and social practices—for example economic, social, political or cultural—to take place on a geographic scale that transcends three or more national jurisdictions.[4] At minimum, such a structure should fulfill several criteria. Firstly, it must have a means to receive and impart communications, both within its structural components and between the structural whole and other institutions or organizations. Secondly, as a corollary of the first, it must be able to integrate the subunits that make up the structural whole. Thirdly, there must be some notion of the constituted whole, that is: what constitutes the 'we' who make up the transnational organization? Lastly, the organizational structure needs to be able to conjure the requisite self-knowledge in order for its members to be able to collectively understand the organization's past and plan for its future. Conventionally speaking, *international* organizations have been divided into two types.[5] On the one hand are inter-governmental organizations (IGOs) and on the other are non-governmental organizations (NGOs). This distinction is particularly important in understanding the historical genesis and development of Interpol, as will be discussed below. Theories and debates about the nature of international organization are abundant. At issue is the nature of globalization and the international state system and, relatedly, the sovereignty of the state. Transnational organizations, of which Interpol is an example, operate at arms length from the international system of states and are independent of any particular state's sovereign claims.

Because of its challenging relationship to the notion of state sovereignty, transnational law is a difficult concept to theorize. While sociologists have traced empirically the emergence of the global networked society the terminology surrounding it remains often ill-defined. The same can be said for legal theory so, whilst Cotterrell argued that transnational law "remains an imprecise notion" he nevertheless states that "it can be confidently predicted that the transnational extension and transformation of law will become ever more clearly one of the most urgent and practically important *foci* for systematic

4 See Castells, M. (1996–2004)—*The Information Age: Economy, Society and Culture* 1996–1998, 2000–2004 editions, Oxford: Blackwell; Vol. 1 *The Rise of the Network Society* (1996, 2nd ed. 2000); Vol. 2 *The Power of Identity* (1997, 2nd ed. 2004); Vol. 3 *End of the Millennium* (1998, 2nd ed. 2000) and Sklair, L. (1995) *The Sociology of the Global System*, Baltimore: Johns Hopkins University press; Sklair, L. (2007) 'A Transnational Framework for Theory and Research in the Study of Globalization' in *Frontiers of Globalization Research; Theoretical and Methodological Approaches* Ino Rossi (ed.) New York NY: Springer, pp. 93–308, for detailed consideration of the concept 'transnational practices'.

5 Groom, A.J.R. (1978) 'The Advent of International Institutions' in *International Organization: A Conceptual Approach*, Paul Taylor and A.J.R. Goom (eds.) London: Pinter pp. 11–27.

inquiry by sociolegal researchers, as well as for the ingenuity of lawyers, legal scholars, governance experts and regulators".[6] In a world going global, the term 'international law' was found wanting and in 1956 Jessup introduced the term 'transnational law' "to include all law which regulates actions or events that transcend national frontiers."[7] He specified that both "public and private international law are included, as are other rules which do not wholly fit into such standard categories".[8] Later, in 1969, Jenks summed up the problem for international lawyers when 'the world becomes one':

> The pattern affects every phase of modern life. Political forces interact upon each other throughout the world. Ideological conflict overleaps all frontiers. Strategy has become global. In industry and commerce, transport and finance, the organizational structure of economic life has become international to the point at which it eludes any possibility of effective national control. Science, though constricted by security controls, owns no instinctive allegiance to anything but the freedom of the mind.[9]

The problem that Jessup defined was that, although the world was one, there remained clear complications resulting from the existence of parallel legal systems. This raises a host of theoretical questions.[10] Since law that transcends

6 Cotterrell, Roger (2012) 'What is Transnational Law?' *Law and Social Inquiry*, Vol. 37, No. 2, pp. 500–524, at p. 522.

7 Jessup, Philip C. (1956) *Transnational Law*, New Haven; CT: Yale University Press, p. 2.

8 Ibid., p. 2.

9 Jenks. C.W. (1969) *A New World of Law? A Study of the creative imagination in international law*, London: Harlow.

10 Boister, Neil (2003) '"Transnational Criminal Law"?' *European Journal of International Law*, Vol. 14 No. 5, pp. 953–976; Boister, Neil (2012) *An Introduction to Transnational Criminal Law*, Oxford: Oxford University Press; Halliday, and Shaffer, op cit, ff. 1; Kingsbury, Benedict, Krisch, Nico and Steward, Richard B. (2005) 'The Emergence of Global Administrative Law, *Law and Contemporary Problems*, Vol. 68 pp. 15–61; Tamanaha, B.Z. (2008) 'Understanding Legal Pluralism: past to Present, Local to Global' *Sydney Law Review*, Vol. 30 pp. 375–411; Tamanaha, Brian, Z. (2015) 'What is Law?' Washington University in St. Louis Legal Studies Research Paper No. 15-01-01, Jan. 7th 2015 http://papers.ssrn.com/sol3/Papers.cfm?abstract_id=2546370## (last visiting April, 2016); Viellechner, L. (2015) 'Review of Transnational Legal Ordering and State Change & Transnational Legal Orders' in *The European Journal of International Law*, Vol. 26 No. 3, pp. 767–793; Walker, Neil (2008) 'Taking Constitutionalism Beyond the State' *Political Studies* Vol. 56, pp. 519–543; Wiener, Antje, Lang, Anthony F. Tully, James, Poiares, Migeul Maduro and Kumm, Mattias (2012) 'Global Constitutionalism: Human Rights, Democracy and the Rule of Law' in Global Constitutionalism, Vol. 1, pp. 1–15.

national frontiers necessarily moves beyond territorially bound definitions of legal sovereignty, upon what does its authority rest? If legitimate authority depends on the presence of democratic representatives who ensure that law is made in the public interest, transnational law which transcends that of the international system of states presents certain challenges to notions of political and legal accountability since it is beyond the control of 'normal' (domestic) politics. Further, if law is judged on the basis of its evident fairness and justice in the eye of the public, it can be difficult to see how transnational law and a relevant public are so mediated. The transnational perspective on global society poses questions of accountability, inclusiveness, and the practical definition of law in global public administration. At a stretch, it even raises the ultimate question in legal theory—'what is law?'—and it certainly points to concerns about law's relationship with democracy and human rights. All of this warrants further exploration, not least because most considerations of law under conditions of transnationalisation lack empirical grounding.[11] This paper has a focused concern with the transnational organization of transnational policing under the auspices of Interpol. Through an empirical uncovering of some of its most salient institutional practices the essay seeks to cast light on more general concerns about the relationship between transnational organization and transnational law in the constitution of a transnational legal order. The empirical discussion provides grounds for abstract and theoretical claims about the nature of law under transnational conditions.

Global policing practice offers a unique window onto the transnational practices that constitute the emerging global system. The transnational practices of police agencies are a particularly interesting example of the sociology of the global system because policing is central to social order. Global policing is a synecdoche of global governance.[12] It follows that an examination of transnational police organization and the transnational legal practices that such may undertake would offer important clues not only to the nature of the evolving global system, but also to the specificities of transnational organization and transnational law. A case in point is the Interpol Red Notice, which has been described as "the cornerstone of international policing".[13] According to Martha, a "Red Notice essentially advises police worldwide that a certain person is wanted and requests members to assist the organisation [Interpol] in apprehending the wanted person on behalf of the requesting country".[14]

---

11 Op. cit., Viellechner, 2015, ff. 10, p. 768.

12 Op. cit., Bowling and Sheptycki, (2012) ff. 2.

13 Martha, Rutsel Silvestre J. (2010) *The Legal Foundations of Interpol*, Oxford; Hart, p. 28.

14 Ibid. p. 28.

This anodyne statement is a remarkable one because it refers to the power of arrest—an exercise of power that deprives a person of liberty. Facilitating such activity on a world-wide basis counts as a transnational practice, and it raises important questions about the transnational legal order of global policing. The mere issuance of a Red Notice need not result in police action, it must be emphasized, since they are not commands. When a local police National Central Bureau (NCB) in country X issues a notice of some kind via the Interpol communications system, receiving Interpol NCBs in other countries retain a capacity to decide how to respond to the request based on the legal instruments at their disposal. In some places local judicial authorities also retain subsidiary legal power tools that can shape local responses. There is a legal grey area, where the transnational organization of Interpol reflects, penetrates and harnesses national law and legal institutions to its own organizational project and that of the transnational legal order of global policing. One evident effect of the Red Notice system happens at international borders where being 'flagged' within the Interpol system makes transnational travel risky for some.[15]

1 The Constitution of Interpol

Thinking transnationally about law takes constitutionalism 'beyond the State'.[16] Further 'global constitutionalism' beyond the state raises fundamental questions about democracy and human rights and their relation to law under transnational conditions.[17] Interpol can be understood as a transnational organization and offers an empirical case study in the global application of administrative law.[18] "Interpol is a dubious legal object".[19] The original idea for Interpol predates the First World War, but its development as a network of national police officials, the International Criminal Police Commission

15 Boycott, Owen (2013) 'Interpol accused of failing to scrutinize red notice requests' *The Guardian*, Wed. Nov. 27, 2013; De Schutter, B. (2002) 'Police information Exchange and Privacy Protection; a European Perspective' in *Strategies of the EU and the US in Combating Transnational Organized Crime*, Brice de Ruyver, Gert Vermeulen and Tom Vander Beken (eds.) Ghent University: Institute for International Research on Criminal Policy, pp. 79–89; Fair Trials International (2013) *Strengthening respect for human rights, strengthening INTERPOL*, London: Fair Trials International, Registered Charity No. 1134586.

16 Op. cit. Walker, ff. 10.

17 Op. cit. Wiener, et al. ff 10.

18 Op. cit. Kingsbury et al., 2005, ff. 10.

19 Savino, Mario (2011) "Global Administrative Law Meets 'Soft' Powers: The Uncomforable Case of Interpol Red Notices", *International Law and Politics*, Vol. 43, pp. 263–336, p. 263.

(ICPC), really began in the interwar period.[20] Prior to the Second World War, the ICPC was under Austrian domination and was based on an agreement between police officers of 22 countries (mostly European, with the involvement of the United States' FBI). After fifteen years of Austrian administration, both in terms of funding and personnel, the ICPC fell under a period of Nazi domination and the HQ was moved to Berlin.[21] The organization was revived in 1946 and its Headquarters was moved to Saint-Cloud a suburb of Paris. The existing Interpol Constitution was first adopted in 1956. The subsequent history of Interpol as a transnational organization has been shaped by the need to appear 'politically neutral'. Articles 2 and 3 of its Constitution are considered most important in this regard.[22] According to Article 2 of that document, the aims of the organization are

1. To facilitate international police co-operation within the limits of existing laws in different countries and in the spirit of the Universal Declaration of Human Rights
2. To establish and develop institutions likely to contribute to the prevention and suppression of ordinary law crimes

The concept of 'ordinary law crime' is vitally important but the meaning of the term is unclear. In the French version of the Interpol Constitution the phrase used is *"criminalité de droit commun".* The term is not particularly common parlance in either language. The terminology is an attempt to bracket off those sorts of illegalities that are said to be 'political' in nature. Article 3 of the Interpol Constitution stipulates that "[I]t is strictly forbidden for the Organization to undertake any intervention or activities of a political, military, religious or racial character". Again, there are differences between the French and English versions. The French version of Article 3 states: *"Toute activite ou intervention dans des questions ou affaires presentant un caractere politique, militaire, religieux ou racial est rigouresusement interdite a l'Organisation."* The difference between the English and French versions is significant, because

---

20 Deflem, M. (2003) *Policing World Society; Historical foundations of International Police Cooperation*, Oxford: Clarendon.

21 Deflem, M. (2002) "The logic of Nazification: The Case of the International Criminal Police Commission ('Interpol')" *International Journal of Comparative Sociology* Vol. 43 No. 1, pp. 21–44.

22 Sheptycki, James (2004) The Accountability of Transnational Policing Institutions: The Strange Case of Interpol, *Canadian Journal of Law and Society*, Vol. 19 no. 1, pp. 107–134, see esp. pp. 127–132.

the political and otherwise 'character' does not relate to the same thing. In the English version it relates to activities of the organization itself, which are forbidden if and when they acquire these characteristics. In the French version, it is the matters which the organization might be called on to intervene in which are the object. The drafters of the Constitution were trying to indicate that Interpol intended to facilitate police co-operation with regard to crimes that were somehow *mala in se* and not crime so defined because of some form of political persecution. Leaving aside the difficult matter of 'ordinary law crime status' that Interpol ascribes to activities because of 'drug prohibition'[23]—which are arguably not *mala in se* but rather *mala prohibita*, and thus political—the 'ordinary law crime/political crime' distinction has raised practical difficulties of interpretation for Interpol in many instances.[24]

It is notable that discussions about Interpol membership frequently refer to 'countries' (not 'states'), because it is police agencies that are members and not the states in which they are embedded. The controversial constitutional history of Interpol follows its organization in parallel and interactively reinforces its evolution and emergence as a transnational organization.[25] Interpol first gained international recognition via the back door when it persuaded the League of Nations to recognize it as the official 'Agency of Fulfillment' for the 1929 Convention on Currency Counterfeiting.[26] According to Anderson, despite the lack of an initial formal treaty basis the organization gradually became recognized as a public international organization.[27] Interpol applied to the UN for the status of Non-Governmental Organization, which was granted in 1948. In 1971 a special arrangement was made with the UN such that Interpol was treated *as if* it were an Intergovernmental Organization. Subsequent to that time the organization participated in various UN committees and Council of Europe business and gained formal mention in a number of international treaties concerning mutual legal assistance.

---

23 Nadelmann, E. (1990) 'Global Prohibition Regimes; the evolution of norms in international society' *International Organization*, Vol. 44 No. 4, pp. 479–526.

24 Anderson, Malcolm (1989) *Policing the World Interpol and the Politics of International Police Co-operation*, Oxford: Oxford University Press; Bressler, F. (1992) *Interpol*, London: Sinclair-Stevenson; Bromund, Ted, R. and Kopel, David B. (2013) *Backgrounder: Necessary Reforms Can Keep Interpol Working in the U.S. Interest*, Washington DC: The Heritage Foundation Vo. 2861 Dec. 11, 2013 Fooner, M. (1989) *Interpol; issues in world crime and international justice*, New York, Plenum Press.

25 Op. cit. Savino, ff. 19, pp. 271–272; op. cit. Sheptycki, 2004, ff. 21 pp. 217–23.

26 Op. cit. Fooner, ff. 24, p. 52.

27 Op. cit. Anderson 1989, ff. 24.

International legal scholar Rustle Silvestre Martha, at one time head of the Interpol Office of Legal Affairs, has argued that the legal basis of Interpol comes down to a question of "how to establish whether the consensus of wills reflected in Interpol's constitution can be attributed to the countries of those officers who participated in its adoption and continue to participate in its activities". He suggests that precedent exists such that "even the *procés-verbal* of an international conference forms an adequate record of an informal agreement."[28] He argues that documents such as the 1923 foundational ones, the 1956 Headquarters Agreement with France and affirmation of the new Interpol Constitution in the early 21st century and even member countries annual (re)confirmation of financial contributions all indicate that Interpol membership is based on the will of member countries.[29] Over time then, "Interpol accrued something like customary status as an IGO".[30] It has typical attributes of an International Governmental Organization: a permanent institutional base (its Headquarters situated in Lyon, France since 1984), a decision-making body (the General Assembly with, currently, 190 members), an administrative body (the General Secretariat situated in the Lyon HQ) and an Executive Committee (for day-to-day management). Additionally, Interpol has field offices in each member country (National Central Bureaux, NCBs). Formally speaking, Interpol fulfills all four criteria in order to count as a transnational organization: First, it has the means to receive and impart communications, both within its structural components and between the structural whole and other institutions or organizations. Second, by means of the NCB network, it is able to integrate subunits that make up a structural whole. Third, by means of its bureaucratic organization there is a practically functioning membership which constitutes a 'we' who 'make up' the institution. Lastly, the organizational structure does conjure institutional self-knowledge and on that basis is able to understand its past and plan for its future. A clear example of this was the establishment of the Commission for the Control of Interpol's Files (CCF) under the terms of a new Headquarters Agreement in 2009, as this paper will go on to explain.

In March of 2008 Martha, then acting as Interpol's General Legal Counsel, wrote to the UN Secretariat requesting consideration of the Interpol Constitution as to whether that document qualified as an international treaty and, as such, if it qualified for registration as an intergovernmental organization with the United Nations. In reply, Nicholas Michel—the UN Under-Secretary

28 Op. cit. Martha, 2010, ff. 13 pp. 150–51.

29 Ibid., p. 164.

30 Op. cit. Sheptycki, 2004, ff. 22, p. 120.

for Legal Affairs—wrote that whether or not the Constitution had been intended as a treaty in the first instance was less important that the character it had acquired over time and that he had no doubt that Interpol was recognized as an IGO.[31] He did however, leave some room for maneuver in saying that acceptance of an instrument for formal registration did not confer "the status of a treaty or international agreement if it does not already possess that status".[32] Following Michel's suggestion the Interpol General Assembly adopted a resolution agreeing that the existing Constitution should be considered an international agreement (i.e. a Treaty) and voted in favour of submitting it for publication by the UN Secretariat. Subsequent publication would enter the Interpol Constitution into the permanent UN record as a treaty providing confirmation that it is an IGO.[33]

However, although Interpol presents as an IGO, in its actual functioning it appears more as an informal network of police bureaucrats. That is, Interpol is not so much *inter*-governmental, as it is *trans*-national. In this respect, the networks that comprise and underpin the formal Interpol structure are of 'sub-state actors' (ie. police bureaucrats) acting transnationally and under conditions of low visibility.[34] Decisions made within Interpol are made by police bureaucrats rather than high-ranking diplomatic officials, or other formal 'high level' states' representatives, and there is no external oversight. Police delegations and Interpol employees gather together at Interpol meetings (up to and including the General Assembly) to discuss strategy, tactics, procedures and processes relating to transnational policing practices. Interpol NCBs are subject to their respective domestic laws, but act as extensions of Interpol. In so doing, they implement Interpol decisions; collect data that feed Interpol databases (subject only to an internal system of audit at HQ and not to any external purview); exchange intelligence and information in a permanent dialogue with other members; and contribute to the symbolic representation of police anti-crime action as de-politicized and neutral. This later point is crucial because Article 3 of the Interpol Constitution forbids "activities of a political, military, religious or racial character". Because of this stated neutrality, almost all countries of the world—regardless of and despite political make-up, religious affiliations, ideological divisions etc.—are able to co-operate in police matters

31 Michel, Nicholas, *Letter of the United Nations' Under-Secretary General for Legal Affairs*, dated May 6th, 2008; Appendix I AG-2011-Res-15 Hanoi: Interpol 2011.

32 Ibid.

33 Stalcup, M. 'Interpol and the emergence of Global Policing' in *Policing and Contemporary Governance*, William Garriott (ed.) New York: Palgrave Macmillan 2013 237.

34 Op. cit. Bowling and Sheptycki, 2012, ff. 2 pp. 36–39.

on the *assumption* that the ends of Interpol are not politically motivated but are merely functionally oriented towards 'ordinary law crime control'. The appearance of neutrality is "both illusory and cogent".[35] Interpol cannot be apolitical because no police institution is. There remains an essential ambiguity in the legal functioning and practices of Interpol and the appearance of neutrality is important for maintaining the legitimacy of 'the brand'.[36]

II The Commission for the Control of Interpol's Files

Cheah Wui Ling, a legal scholar at the National University of Singapore and formerly a Legal Officer at Interpol's General Secretariat, has described the Commission for the Control of Interpol's Files (CCF). She describes a strictly internalized regime of legal accountability.[37] According to her, nothing like it existed before it was created in 2008. It was created out of the recognition that, because of Interpol's success in the first decade of the 21st century, "the organization has come under increased scrutiny and has faced attempted lawsuits by individuals".[38] The new Headquarters Agreement of 2009 established the CCF to "be governed solely by Interpol's legal order, confirming that Commission's status as an organ of Interpol".[39] Article 36 of Interpol's amended Constitution expressly recognizes the CCF as "an independent body" that "shall ensure the processing of personal information by the Organization is in compliance with the regulations the Organization establishes in this matter".[40] However, "the Constitution does not detail how the Commission shall 'ensure' Interpol's compliance with its data processing rules" (p. 388) but the CCF's "composition and its functioning shall be subject to specific rules to be laid down by the [Interpol] General Assembly".[41] In other words, the CCF is subject to the internal accountability mechanisms of Interpol itself with the General Assembly acting as court of last resort in the event of disagreements between the General Secretariat and the Commission for the Control of Interpol's Files.

---

35 Op. cit. Savino, ff. 19, p. 280.

36 Sheptycki, J. 'Brand Interpol' in *Trust in International Police and Justice Cooperation*, Saskia Hufnagel and Carol McCartney (eds.) Oxford: Hart Publishing 2017.

37 Cheah, Wui Ling, (2010) 'Policing Interpol: The Commission for the Control of Interpol's Files and the Right to Remedy', *International Organizations Law Review* Vol. 7, 2010 379.

38 Ibid. p. 378.

39 Ibid. pp. 387–88.

40 Ibid. p. 388.

41 Ibid. p. 388.

The remedies provided by the CCF are intended to protect against the possible eventuality of legal action by individuals negatively affected by Interpol actions (such as the issuance of a Red Notice that is somehow inappropriate).

Here again is an example of Interpol using legal instruments in order to constitute itself as a transnational organization. In this instance, it is about protecting the organization from private legal actions. According to Cheah, it "seems only fair that individuals affected by IO [International Organization—i.e. Interpol] wrongdoing are able to obtain a remedy".[42] However this is problematic. As a putative organizational subject of transnational legal order, Interpol has obligations beyond that of its constituent members, a fact that is recognized in its own constitution, Article 2 of which requires the organizations work to be conducted "in the spirit of the Universal Declaration of Human Rights".[43] The interests of individual Interpol members may conflict with larger organizational interests with respect to Red Notices. Actions undertaken under the auspices of Interpol are obligated to respect human rights law. The enforcement of such an obligation is problematic, as Cheah notes, because domestic courts are generally unable to hear individual claims against International Organizations and such organizations are usually immune from such suits either as a result of specific treaty requirements or as a result of customary international law. However, as Cheah also notes, "domestic and regional courts have increasingly demonstrated a willingness to ignore IO immunity".[44] The establishment of the CCF was therefore a buffer intended to protect against the possibility of private legal action. The presumed threat was that, if no such remedial body existed, domestic courts might decide to ignore the customary legal immunities of a formally designated International Organization like Interpol so as to provide an individual with a remedy in the event that a tort or violation of human rights could be argued. Noting that "the CCF does not have the benefit of external judicial review" a report by *Fair Trials International* remarked the arrangement provides "no authority capable of ensuring that the rule of law is adhered to". The report concludes that the CCF "falls far short of basic standards of fairness, effectiveness and independence." "In light of these shortcomings", it goes on to say, "Interpol's judicial immunity is currently unjustifiable.[45]

42 Ibid. p. 379.

43 Ibid. p. 384.

44 Ibid. p. 379.

45 Op. cit. Fair Trials International, 2013, ff. 15 p. 60.

III Interpol Organization and the Red Notice System

Interpol functions as part of a complex web of global police communications. It facilitates the transmission of police-to-police communication between member agencies. However, "The man from Interpol never arrested anyone".[46] Interpol's primary function is the exchange of messages—for example requests for information about a given person's criminal history or requests that enquiries be undertaken—between police authorities in member countries. The quickest method is a so-called 'diffusion', issued by member countries and circulated without formal review by Interpol HQ. Frequently these are followed up with a 'formal notice', the system of coloured notices. Red Notices facilitate the worldwide circulation of arrest warrants issued by domestic authorities in the country of origin; Blue are specific requests for information on named persons of interest in relation to a crime; Green circulate information and intelligence of suspect individuals and activities; Orange relate to hazardous materials or other potential threats to public safety; Yellow relate to missing persons; and Black Notices report unidentified dead bodies. In 2005 the UN-Interpol 'Special Notice' was introduced. Issued jointly by the UN Security Council and Interpol, these Special Notices pertain to groups and individuals associated with international terrorism.[47] Interpol maintains separate databases relating to stolen and lost travel documents, stolen motor vehicles, fingerprints, DNA, 'habitual criminals', child sex offenders, without external oversight. As well as facilitating police-to-police communications, Interpol provides three other basic functions: database maintenance and intelligence analysis; operational support; and training. The circulation of Red Notices is one small but important example of the capabilities of the Interpol organization.

Notices are circulated to members through the system of National Central Bureaux (NCBs) administered under Interpol's Rules on the Processing of Information (RPI) for the purpose of international police co-operation. Article 1(1) defines notices as 'international INTERPOL notifications containing sets of information recorded in the police information system and circulated by the General Secretariat, for the purposes referred to in Article 3.1.(a)'. Notices are thus considered acts of the organization itself, facilitating requests issued by a particular NCB. Notices can be divided into two types: requests for action and alerts. Notices requesting a police intervention can be published in

46 Op. cit. Sheptycki, 2004, ff. 22 p. 116.

47 Deflem M. and Maybin, Lindsay C. 'Interpol and the Policing of International Terrorism; Developments and Dynamics since September 11' in *Terrorism: Research, Readings and Realities*, Lynne L. Snowden and Brad Whitsel (eds.) New York: Prentice Hall, 2005.

order to: search for a person with a view to arrest; obtain information about a person who has committed or is likely to commit, or participated or likely to have participated in the commission of a crime; locate a missing person; locate a witness or victim; identify a person or a dead body; and locate or identify objects. Notices amounting to alerts are published through Interpol channels and on its website in order to warn police authorities about a person's criminal activities, to describe *modus operandi* or offences committed by unidentified persons, characteristics of counterfeits or forgeries and the seizure of items in connection with anti-trafficking operations. Any notice containing a request for action triggers Article 31 of the Interpol Constitution which calls upon members to exercise constant and active co-operation and to do all within their power, commensurate with domestic legislation, in order to participate diligently in Interpol activities.[48] There nonetheless remains discretion at the local level and there is no organizational sanction against inaction.

The issuance of a Red Notice presupposes the establishment of police databases and a communications infrastructure linking them, which has implications for the individual right to privacy and informational self-determination.[49] Interpol's world-wide communications system is called I-Link.[50] Interpol's rules on the processing of police information focus on control of personal data and regulate concerns about privacy and data protection. Red Notices concern persons that are wanted by national jurisdictions or by international organizations (e.g. international criminal tribunals). As recently as 1998 Interpol circulated only 737 Red Notices. According to the Interpol Annual Report for 2011, a total of 6,344 Red Notices were issued in the previous year, an increase of more than twenty-six percent on the previous year's issuance of 5,020. This figure was a marked increase of sixty-one percent from 2008.[51] According to a report issued by the US based Heritage Foundation 'think tank' in 2013, in 2011 Interpol issued over 10 thousand notices, of which 7,678 were Red Notices.[52] The acceleration Interpol Red Notice issuance has been enabled by new computer and communications technologies—a common experience across policing institutions globally. In 2017, the Interpol Office of Communications published a 'fact sheet' which indicated that a total of 12,878 Red Notices and 26,645

48 Martha, Rutsel Silvestre J. 'Challenging Acts of Interpol in Domestic Courts' in *Challenging Acts of International Organizations Before Domestic Courts*, August Reinisch (ed.) Oxford: Oxford University Press 2010.

49 Op. cit. De Schutter, 2002 ff. 15.

50 Op. cit. Stalcup, ff. 33 2013. p. 242.

51 Op. cit. Savino, 2011, ff. 19 p. 287.

52 Op. cit. Bromund and Kopel, 2013 ff. 24.

Diffusions were issued out of a total of 47,451 notices circulated world wide (a figure which includes 33 individuals and entities associated with Al Qaeda and the Taliban).[53]

As explained previously, "Interpol has invested much into developing the Commission for the Control of Interpol's Files ... as an independent remedial body".[54] Under Article 2 of the Interpol Constitution, when members undertake action in response to Red Notices they do so under the auspices of their own domestic laws, not Interpol rules. According to Article 2.2 of the Constitution, in general the organization's aims are to "ensure and promote the widest possible mutual assistance between all criminal police authorities within the limits of the laws existing in the different countries and in the spirit of the Universal Declaration of Human Rights".[55] According to the Rules on the Processes of Information for the Purposes of International Police Co-operation (hereafter RPI), data provided for circulation by Interpol from "a National Central Bureau, an authorized national institution, or authorized international entity" is considered "*a priori* to be accurate and relevant" and that the General Secretariat can facilitate its circulation in good faith subject to the proviso that the data processed conforms to Interpol rules.[56] The matter might seem clear cut, but actually this is a grey zone of responsibility because it is the members who "own the data" not the organization. In view of this, the rules both require the members themselves to ensure that data submitted for processing complies with them and gives responsibility to the Secretariat to remind members of their obligations. "In other words, there is an overlapping of responsibilities between the General Secretariat and Interpol members who own the data concerned".[57] With respect to the information circulated in Red Notice Requests, Article 10.I.d of the RPI requires the General Secretariat to respect "the basic rights of individuals the information concerns" while taking "all appropriate steps" to prevent any prejudice to members and the

---

53 Interpol Fact Sheet, *The International Notices System*, Interpol HQ, Lyon, France COM/FS/2017-02/GI-02.

54 Op. cit. Cheah, 2010 ff. 38 p. 379.

55 ICPO-INTERPOL Constitution art. 2(1). The Constitution was adopted in 1956 and last amended in 2008. ICPO-INTERPOL Constitution and General Regulations, INTERPOL, http://www.interpol.int/Public/ICPO/LegalMaterials/constitution/constitutionGenReg/constitution.asp#amd (last visited April, 2016).

56 Rules on the Processing of Information for the Purposes of International Police Co-operation, adopted by General Assembly Resolution AG-2003-RES-04 available at www.interpol.int.

57 Op. cit. Cheah, 2010 ff. 38 p. 383.

organization.[58] This ambiguity exists in a transnational administrative grey zone of the putative 'international' system of states.

The RPIs are the legal tools that allow for the circulation of Red Notices (and other types of notices). The tools require that, before publishing notices, the General Secretariat must assess whether it is advisable to do so in the light of Articles 2 and 3 of the Constitution "bearing in mind the risks run to international police co-operation, the Organization, its staff, and its member countries".[59] These rules require that a requesting NCB must ensure that

- the person sought is the subject of criminal proceedings or has been convicted of a crime, and references to an enforceable arrest warrant, court decision or other judicial documents are provided;
- assurances have been given that extradition will be sought upon arrest of the person in conformity with national laws and/or the applicable bilateral and multilateral treaties;
- sufficient information is provided to allow for the co-operation requested to be effective.[60]

Furthermore, the Implementing Rules stipulate that before "publishing and circulating a notice at its own initiative, the General Secretariat shall ensure that the conditions attached to the given notice are met".[61] However, the grey zone of responsibility lies in the fact that there does not appear to be a process for independent verification by the Organization of the actual information contained in a circulated Red Notice. The Rules state that:

> The General Secretariat may only publish a notice once it has verified that the processing required conforms to the rules in force and once the National Central Bureau, authorized national institution or authorized international entity which requested its publication, has communicated to it all the required sets of information[62]

Interpol operations are based on the presumption that police are acting with complete integrity. Speaking in a meeting of Interpol Heads of NCBs in 2007, then Interpol Secretary General Ron Noble stated that "it is our presumption

58 Ibid. p. 384.
59 Op. cit. ICPO-INTERPOL Constitution ff. 55 art. 10.5(b).
60 Ibid. art. 37(a)1(ii).
61 Ibid. art. 37(b).
62 Op. cit. Cheah, 2010 ff. 38 p. 383.

that a country requesting a Red Notice is acting in accord with Interpol policy".[63] According to Yaron Gottlieb, acting as Interpol's Senior Legal Counsel, the organization assumes

> that what we receive here is accurate and relevant [and] that an arrest warrant is issued by a judge who is not corrupt ... that the case is not political ... if we receive information or if we have our own information—that in fact, the case is different from what it seems to be—we engage in a full review.[64]

The system, as described by Gottlieb, Cheah and others, is cumbersome and works on a case-by-case basis. The ability of Interpol to proactively undertake the vetting of Red Notice requests has declined as the volume of such requests has increased. According to Cheah, while members are required to ensure that information submitted conforms to the Organization's rules, subsequent checks are largely concerned with the validity of the request, not the underlying factual basis of them.[65] Interpol does not have the investigative powers to undertake such factual checks, its role is to facilitate the requests of its member agencies. Since the Interpol I-Link system has automated the Red Notice process they are now entered into the system directly by member agencies themselves and other member agencies see them before a formal process of review is undertaken by Interpol itself.[66]

In the opinion of Anand Doobay, a UK-based lawyer who has represented people who have been made the subject of Red Notices, the process is unfair:

> There is no transparency to it. It's weighted in favour of law enforcement and the need to prevent and disrupt serious crime and terrorism. There is very little by way of protection to keep the state—or even one corrupt prosecutor—from misusing the process.[67]

This point is reiterated by Phillippe Neyroud, a Geneva-based lawyer who has similarly defended people on the Red Notice list. He observes that Interpol is not subject to any outside oversight: "So when there's an abuse, there's almost

63 Op. cit. Stalcup, 2013, ff. 33 p. 242.
64 Op. cit. Lewis 2010, ff. 54.
65 Op. cit. Cheah, 2010 ff. 38 pp. 385–87.
66 Op cit. Stalcup, 2013, ff. 33 p. 242; op. cit., Lewis, 2011, ff. 50.
67 Quoted in Lewis 2011, ff. 54.

no remedy".[68] In 2010 the *International Consortium of Investigative Journalists* (ICIJ) analyzed a sample of 7622 Interpol Red Notices issued by 145 different countries' police agencies, finding that about twenty-five percent emanated from countries which, according to *Freedom House*, had severe restrictions of political rights and civil liberties and that half emanated from countries deemed corrupt by *Transparency International*.[69] A Report by *Fair Trials International* in 2013 detailed seventeen seriously problematic Red Notices.[70] In one instance the Red Notice referred to a group of twelve Kurds naturalized as Swedish (EU) citizens who were the subject of an Interpol notice originating from Iran based on terrorism related matters. Another example was that of Estonian Anastasia Rybachenko, a social activist in the 'Solidarnost movement' who was made the subject of a Red Notice on the basis of allegations of participation in 'mass rioting'. Yet another is of Wadih Sagheih, a trader in precious stones and jewelry who was falsely accused of fraud in Abu Dhabi and thereby made subject of another Interpol Red Notice. During the writing of this essay, Bill Browder a US-born British citizen and high-profile global critic of Vladimir Putin, was the subject of an Interpol diffusion, putting his ability to travel internationally at risk.[71] Keeping in mind the increasing volume of Red Notice requests, the CCF vetting process, which proceeds on a case-by-case basis, is a structural hurdle that gets in the way of facilitating police co-operation.[72] Observation suggests that the pressure of organizational efficiency overwhelms the capacity of the CCF to proactively review files.[73] The result leaves the 'bad' global citizen at risk of being 'stripped naked' and confined in a transnational penal space.[74]

68 Ibid.

69 Lewis, L. 'Interpol's Red Notices used by some to pursue political dissenters, opponents' *International Consortium of Investigative Journalists*, July 20, 2011, at: https://www.icij.org/project/interpols-red-flag/interpols-red-notices-used-some-pursue-political-dissenters-opponents (last visited Nov., 2016).

70 Op. cit. Fair Trials International 2013, ff. 15.

71 Mark Townsend, Russia puts British Putin critic on Interpol wanted list, *The Observer* Sunday Oct. 22, 2017.

72 Op. cit. Lewis 2010, ff. 54.

73 Op. cit. Boycott, 2013 ff. 15; op. cit. Lewis, 2011, ff. 54; Llopis-Jepsen, Celia (2009) 'Why did the NIA bar Dolkun Isa?' *Taipei Times*, Wed. July 22, 2009; Radio Free Asia (2012) 'Activist Allowed to Enter US', Nov. 13, 2012; http://www.rfa.org/english/news/uyghur/dolkun-isa-11132012171203.html; Zeldin, Wendy (2010) 'Interpol Red Notices' *The Law Library of Congress, Global Research Center*, Washington DC.

74 Boister, N. (forthcoming) "The 'bad global citizen', 'naked', in the transnational penal space" in this volume.

The reader might pause to reflect that any analysis of transnational legal orders eventually begs questions about their consequences, especially those affecting the institutionalization of global legal norms more generally.[75] The example of the constitution of Interpol and the deployment of one of its principle legal tools provides an empirical case study in transnational law making in which international, national, and local processes are brought into interaction contributing to the establishment of a transnational legal order of global policing. Normative questions, especially those having to do with the uneasy results when transnational criminal law instruments impinge on individual rights have been frequently explored in the literature.[76] In the remaining pages of this essay I would like to direct the reader's attention to another kind of higher order reflection about the nature of law under conditions of transnationalisation and focus thinking on how legal tools are used by knowing social actors.

IV Conclusion: Transnational Legal Orders as Transnational Rule with Law

Interpol is a transnational organization that works to constitute a transnational legal order by using legal tools. The discussion pursued here has shown how Interpol constituted itself as a legal entity and maneuvered its institutional status so as to become an International Governmental Organization (IGO). The Constitution of Interpol works to establish its independence in the global system. In the scathing words of the international private lawyer Phillippe Neyroud, "Interpol is not like the United Nations. It is just like the Jockey Club", but fiery rhetoric cannot compensate for the lack of legal tools available to private actors where the transnational legal order of policing is concerned.[77] The discussion of the Red Notice system pursued here gives an empirical reference point for understanding how transnational organization and transnational law work in practice.

In trying to answer the question *What is Law?* Brian Tamanaha concluded that law is a plurality of discourses, collections of social historical phenomena that specific groups of people have collectively recognized as law in different times and places.[78] Elsewhere, he observed that

75 Op. cit. Halliday and Shaffer, 2015, ff. 1 p. 53.

76 M. Wade 'General Principles of Transnational Criminal Justice? Exploratory Reflections' *Utrecht Law Review* Vol. 9 2013, pp. 165ff.

77 Quoted in Lewis, 2011 op. cit. ff. 54.

78 Op. cit. Tamanaha 2015, ff. 10.

> The longstanding vision of a uniform and monopolistic law that governs a community is plainly obsolete ...[but that] official state legal systems, at least those that function effectively, have a distinctive instrumental capacity that enables them to be utilised to engage in a broad (potentially unlimited) range of possible activities ... For those interested in studying law and society, what matters most is framing situations in ways that facilitate the observation and analysis of what appears to be interesting and important.[79]

Interpol is an interesting example of a transnational organization and its use of transnational legal tools—for example, Red Notices—is certainly important. Practically speaking, Interpol is a transnational organization and it might even be an example of what Teubner call law as 'autopoietic system'.[80] Interpol agents wrote themselves into formal legal existence as a transnational organization. Now it is a constituent element in a 'transnational legal order' (TLO). Halliday and Shaffer make the point that "law establishes generalized normative expectations understood and used by actors within a particular context for purposes of constraining and facilitating particular behaviors".[81] Thus, law is a tool.[82] Halliday and Shaffer also observe that "law is constituted by both power and reason".[83] Legal power tools are discursive ones shaped by doctrinal interpretation. Interpol is an empirical manifestation of transnational organization and its working practices show that, while the politics of law is shaped by the internal logic of legal rules, the interpretative use of legal instruments results from acts of political will. The transnational legal order constituted through the organization of Interpol has normative implications for other manifestations of transnational law for example, *inter alia*, global constitutionalism, transnational administrative law, transnational criminal law and international public authority.[84] The empirical example of Interpol offers a litmus test concerning an emerging transnational legal, social, professional and political space that shapes global governance and governance globally and it gives specificity to the theoretical notion of a transnational legal order. Understanding the Red Notice system contributes to socio-legal debates concerning the nature of law

---

79 Op. cit. Tamanaha, 2008, ff. 10. p. 411.

80 Teubner, G. 1993 *Law as an Autopoietic System*, Oxford: Blackwell 1993.

81 Op. cit. Halliday and Shaffer, 2015 ff. 1. p. 11.

82 See also, Bowling and Sheptycki, 2015, ff. 3 and Tamanaha, 2015, ff. 10.

83 Op. cit. Halliday and Shaffer, 2015, ff. 1. p. 17.

84 Op. cit. Boister, 2012; Kingsbury, et al., 2005; Walker, 2008; Wiener et al., 2012, ff. 10.

under transnational conditions drawing attention to a specific transnational organization and the ways in which instruments of legality have been used.

In general, this reveals transnational law as a set of tools—including administrative, constitutional, and criminal law ones—and it illustrates that legal tools are always instruments in the hands of knowing social actors. "When it comes to choices about using legal instruments, claims about effectiveness and efficiency in responding to transnational threats tend to trump claims about democratic legitimacy, human rights and the rule of law".[85] The socio-legal study of the transnational legal order of policing reveals law in this instance to be a set of tools available to a wide variety of policing agents arrayed in a complex global web of interdependence and that private individuals are relatively short of legal instruments to play the game with. Rule following is a social practice set in the context of organizational taken-for-granted knowledge, assumptions and routines. Interpol is an important organizational constituent of the transnational legal order of policing. In that setting practical mastery of legal language is an important social competence. The decision to pick up and deploy legal tools is evidence of the transformative power of legal discourse in which the taken-for-granted knowledge, assumptions and routines of the social world are translated into authoritative terms according to the dictates of the tool users. It is in this sense that law is an instrument in the hands of knowing social actors and the work of police agents in making up their institutional lifeworld largely resides in the mastery of a set of organizational practices and the legal language game which legitimates it. This is an example of rule *with* law.[86]

This is a perhaps a contentious formulation since it challenges the widespread belief in that the international state system is based on the rule *of* law. However, as Boister observes (2012) in the transnational realm, "the system observes rather than develops a rule of law framework".[87] Socio-legal theory recognizes many different conceptions of law and with the empirical example outlined here the notion of rule *with* law is as apt turn of phrase. The empirical example of Interpol is revealing because it is an example of constitutionalism beyond 'the state' and also because it provides a case study in the global application of administrative law. The transnational legal order thus constituted allows its agents to employ domestic legal tools and transnational legal instruments in order to pursue organizational goals and objectives that are global in reach. The discussion here has provided an empirical description of

85 Op. cit. Bowling, B. and Sheptycki, J. (2015) ff. 3 p. 149.

86 Ibid. pp. 155–56.

87 Op. cit. Boister 2003, ff. 10 p. 278.

a transnational organization and the ways in which law has been deployed in the manufacture of a transnational legal order. This empirical case study provides grounding for abstract and theoretical concerns about the nature of law under transnational conditions and thereby a foundation for further consideration of the political and normative dimensions of a world ruled with law.

Acknowledgements

The author owes a debt of gratitude to Mikkel Jarle Chistensen and Neil Boister for their insightful comments on an earlier draft of this paper. Thanks also to Ben Bowling, Paul Swallow, François Tanguay-Renaud, Tanya Alpin, Keith Ewing and Peer Zumbansen for helpful conversations about the topic of the paper during the writing process.

The Social Structure of Transnational Criminal Justice: A Cluster of Spaces beyond National Borders

Mikkel Jarle Christensen
University of Copenhagen, Denmark
mikkel.jarle.christensen@jur.ku.dk

Abstract

This article analyses elements of the social structure of transnational criminal justice. The main goal of the analysis is to investigate if the terminology crafted around transnational criminal law as a distinct legal system corresponds to the social structuration of this space as it can be observed in the justice practices that drive it. To enable such an analysis, the article contributes both a theoretical discussion of how best to conceptualise the social spaces of transnational criminal justice as well as, more cautiously, an empirical investigation into the workings of these spaces, focusing the fight against drugs, terrorism, corruption and ecological crimes. Building conceptually on Pierre Bourdieu's field theory, the analytical focal point of the article is the practices of transnational criminal justice and the professionals who are active in this space. This raises crucial questions of how the social practices of transnational criminal justice structures usages and developments of the law. Based on the identification and analysis of four separate but interrelated spaces of practice, the article argues that our theoretical understanding of transnational criminal justice and law needs to be recalibrated to take into account the different ways in which it is mobilised to create either security or good governance.

Keywords

transnational crime – globalisation – sociology of law – drug trafficking – terrorism – corruption – ecological crime

 | DOI 10.1163/9789004365797_006

Introduction

That globalisation has transformed the patterns of crime has become entrenched in scholarly and popular understanding.[1] To many commentators, this development was closely related to the liberalisation and internationalisation of trade and commerce that accelerated in the 1990s.[2] The very broad terminology crafted around the notion of globalisation highlights ways in which previously disparate nations and communities were tied together by transnational transactions that drove the economy as well as increasingly formatted new forms of transversal social exchanges between professionals, activists, politicians and private individuals.[3]

As a part of this wider transformation, new forms of law were developed beyond the control of any single state, but influenced by the power of large geopolitical powers such as the US and, increasingly, China. The new terrain of international law[4] that has developed since the 1990s took many different directions and affected human rights, international commercial law and arbitration, regional legal structures and institutions as well as criminal law initiatives. Perhaps most striking, and certainly one of the most discussed topics in the scholarly literature,[5] was the development of a new field of international criminal law and justice,[6] centred around the international criminal courts which opened from the mid 1990s.[7] While the innovations of this field (in particular the creation of the International Criminal Court (ICC) established by the Rome Statute in 1998) are certainly important elements in the attempt to secure the prosecution of genocide, crimes against humanity, war crimes

1 Katja Franko Aas, *Globalization & Crime* (9781412912907, Sage Publications 2007).

2 David Held and others, 'Global transformations' (Washington) 22 ReVision 7.

3 Frank J. Lechner and John Boli, *World Culture: origins and consequences* (Blackwell 2005).

4 Karen J. Alter, *The New Terrain of International Law: Courts, Politics, Rights* (Princeton University Press 2014).

5 Elies van Sliedregt, 'International Criminal Law: Over-studied and Underachieving?' 29 *Leiden Journal of International Law* 1.

6 John Hagan and Ron Levi, 'Crimes of War and the Force of Law' 83 Social Forces 1499; Peter Dixon and Chris Tenove, 'International Criminal Justice as a Transnational Field: Rules, Authority and Victims' 7 *International Journal of Transitional Justice* 393; Mikkel Jarle Christensen, 'The Emerging Sociology of International Criminal Courts: Between Global Restructurings and Scientific Innovations' 63 Current Sociology 825.

7 John Hagan, *Justice in the Balkans: Prosecuting War Crimes in the Hague Tribunal* (University of Chicago Press 2003); Mikkel Jarle Christensen, 'From Symbolic Surge to Closing Courts: The Transformation of International Criminal Justice and its Professional Practices' 34 *International Journal of Law, Crime and Justice* 609.

and, potentially, the crime of aggression, these institutions deal with a very limited set of crimes compared to those defined in national criminal codes—even if restricted to the forms of crime that cross borders or have international dimensions.

The composite term 'transnational criminal law' (TCL) was coined to cover crimes that were not codified by international criminal law[8] under a common concept,[9] defining it at the same time as a unified legal 'system'.[10] TCL groups a number of different treaty crimes or private crimes under a common conceptual framework with both an inter-state and a domestic dimension. This article moves the focus away from this legal system to investigate the social, professional and institutional developments that deal with these crimes. As such, the analysis contributes a new perspective on the enforcement mechanisms built around these crimes, and the agents and stakeholders involved in enforcing the law. In other words, the article investigates specific structures of international criminal justice formed around and within the TCL, and impacting its development and the interpretation of its rules. The article will proceed in five sections. First, the theoretical perspective will be briefly outlined alongside the method and empirical material on which the analysis is built. Secondly, the genealogy of TCL as a conceptual product will be outlined by situating its development in the historical context of the 1990s. Thirdly, the article will investigate the social constitution of four forms of transnational criminal justice—drug trafficking, terrorism, corruption and environmental crimes—through a small sample of the elites which are active in these spaces. The conclusion will situate the investigation of transnational criminal justice in a wider space of international governance and point to further research avenues.

1 Theoretical Perspective and Empirical Material

To investigate the social constitution of transnational criminal justice, this section lays out the theoretical framework on which the following analysis will build. The question of how social science can best conceive of and investigate social spaces and their impact has always been at the core of scholarly debates

8 Neil Boister, 'The Exclusion of Treaty Crimes from the Jurisdiction of the Proposed International Criminal Court: Law, Pragmatism, Politics' 3 J Armed Conflict L 27.

9 Neil Boister, 'Transnational Criminal Law?' 14 European Journal of International Law 953.

10 Neil Boister, *An Introduction to Transnational Criminal Law* (0199605386, Oxford University Press 2012).

in this space. A main fault line in these debates has been whether structures or agency is the driving factor in social development.[11] The objectivist (or structuralist) perspective posits that structures, be they social, political or ideological, format the space in which agents act, the work of Karl Marx being a key exponent of this perspective.[12] In the most extreme readings of this objectivist perspective, individual agents have little or no impact on the world of which they are part. In contrast to this point of view, other scholars have conceptualised the relationship between the individual and the world in more subjectivist terms, in which individual capacity and action shapes the world. The most prominent philosophical exponent of this perspective, at least in the French context, was Jean-Paul Sartre,[13] but similar ideas can also be found in rational-choice theories that try to investigate societal problems through an idealised (or rather rationalising) reconstruction of individual (and sometimes collective) action. Central to Bourdieu's project was to reinvigorate social science not only by founding it in rigorous empirical science, but also by theoretically moving beyond the opposition between the objectivist and subjectivist positions.

The core concept developed in Bourdieu's sociology does exactly this. By focusing on the relations that structure specific social spaces, the concept of the field combines the objectivity of these empirically observable connections with the subjective experience of agents as they build strategies to manoeuvre and increase their social and professional value in this space. In other words, while the relations between the different positions of the field are objective, the constant battle to define the stakes of the game—the norms, preferred practices and designation of value in the field—continuously reshapes the field and its internal power dynamics.[14] In addition, internal field dynamics are shaped by the individual and collective competition over material and symbolic resources. At the same time, this social space is influenced by its relation to other fields as well as to larger historical conjunctures. For instance, as Bourdieu showed in the French context, the field of law was structured by specific internal dynamics,[15] but the value of legal work and its practitioners is also shaped by the historical context in which legal professionals operate,[16]

11 Pierre Bourdieu and Loic Wacquant, *An Invitation to Reflexive Sociology* (0226067416, University of Chicago Press 1992) 7.

12 Karl Marx, *Das Kapital, Kritik der politischen Oekonomie* (1867).

13 Jean-Paul Sartre, *L'être et le néant: Essai d'ontologie phe-nomenologique* (Gallimard 1943).

14 Bourdieu and Wacquant 97.

15 Pierre Bourdieu, 'The force of law: toward a sociology of the juridical field' 38 Hastings Law J 805.

16 Pierre Bourdieu, *Sur l'État: Cours au Collège de France 1989–1992* (Seuil 2012) 330.

as well as the social and political economy in which they work and compete with other professionals involved in state governance.[17]

The coexistence of the objective and subjective in Bourdieu's thinking tools is also evident in the core concepts of capital and habitus that are pivotal tools in his sociology. Capital signifies the accumulated expertise and its social value embodied in individual agents that shapes their opportunities in specific fields. This capital, however, only has value if recognised and attributed worth in specific social spaces, something that is often related also to state practices. The state acts as a cardinal point of reference for professional degrees as well as for symbolic construction of what is defined as social and political problems.[18] Similarly, the habitus conceptualises individual accrual of social heritage, experience and life choices that shape the possible positions agents take in social spaces as well as how they perceive and interact with the world. This concept makes the diachronic study of how prestige and positions are inherited possibly as one element in a wider historical investigation of how societal changes transform social practices and, vice versa, how social strategies aim to reshape societal distribution of goods. As such, an agent's habitus is deeply rooted in a historical context in which accumulation of material and symbolic values help shape their outlook and strategies. Something similar could be said about institutional power that also shapes access to power and proximity to state resources. In terms of the law and legal developments, Bourdieu's analysis shows how the field of law is divided into subfields (or specific spaces within these fields as they will be called below) that are attributed with different prestige and offer very different social and material possibilities. As such the historically embedded, and constantly renegotiated, distinctions between different forms of law also formats legal developments as agents in less prestigious legal disciplines, such as social law, adapt practical and symbolic strategies aimed at increasing the recognition of their form of law, and recalibrate the division of power on the national scene.

The field theory has had strong impact beyond the French context in which it was originally developed and has been adapted to the US context[19] as well, even if this circulation meant that it lost parts of its critical reflexivity.[20] Beyond the nation state, the concept of the field has been deployed to study the

---

17 Pierre Bourdieu, *La noblesse d'État* (Éditions de Minuit 1989).

18 Pierre Bourdieu, *Raisons pratiques: sur la théorie de l'action* (Seuil 1994) 107.

19 Neil Fligstein and Doug McAdam, *A Theory of Fields* (9780199859948, Oxford University Press 2012).

20 Yves Dezalay and Mikael Rask Madsen, 'The Force of Law and Lawyers: Pierre Bourdieu and the Reflexive Sociology of Law' 8 Annual Review of Law and Social Science 433.

construction of new international forms of law such as international arbitration,[21] human rights,[22] EU law[23] and international criminal law[24] to name only a few. As part of the transposition of a theoretical tool developed in a national context onto international phenomena that have different characteristics, the concept of the field has been re-examined and discussed in a new light. Most prominently, Christian Topalov's notion of a 'weak field',[25] originally crafted to study specific forms of social organisation in France, has been used to conceptualise the emergence of transnational fields that do not enjoy the same embedded autonomy as those that evolved in close relation to the state, but may very well affect state practices none the less.[26] The existence of weak fields that stretch beyond the state, but often remain structured by state preferences and boundaries, opens up to the central question of how a field is composed and how its borders are drawn vis-à-vis other social spaces. For Bourdieu, the mapping of a field and its boundaries is an empirical rather than a theoretical enterprise, and the field ends where its effects are no longer present. In other words, the fields is fenced in by its social gravity that defines the practices and strategies of the agents active in it and shapes its main narratives and core symbolism that serve to legitimise its practices. In the case of transnational criminal justice, the main question asked in this article is how we can

21 Yves Dezalay and Bryant G. Garth, *Dealing in Virtue: International Commercial Arbitration and the Construction of a Transnational Legal Order* (University of Chicago Press 1996).

22 Mikael Rask Madsen, 'From Cold War Instrument to Supreme European Court: The European Court of Human Rights at the Crossroads of International and National Law and Politics' [Blackwell Publishing Ltd] 32 Law & Social Inquiry 137.

23 Antoine Vauchez, *Brokering Europe: Euro-lawyers and the Making of a Transnational Polity* (9781107042360, Cambridge University Press 2015).

24 John Hagan, Ron Levi and Gabrielle Ferrales, 'Swaying the Hand of Justice: The Internal and External Dynamics of Regime Change at the International Criminal Tribunal for the Former Yugoslavia' [Blackwell Publishing Ltd] 31 Law & Social Inquiry 585; Christensen, 'From Symbolic Surge to Closing Courts: The Transformation of International Criminal Justice and its Professional Practices'.

25 Christian Topalov, *Laboratoires du nouveau siècle: la nébuleuse réformatrice et ses réseaux en France, 1880–1914* (Ecole des hautes études en sciences sociales 1999).

26 Antoine Vauchez, 'Interstitial Power in Fields of Limited Statehood: Introducing a "Weak Field" Approach to the Study of Transnational Settings' [Blackwell Publishing Ltd] 5 International Political Sociology 340; Sara Dezalay, 'Lawyering war or talking peace? On militant usages of the law in the resolution of internal armed conflicts: A case study of International Alert' in Yves Dezalay and Bryant G. Garth (eds), *Lawyers and the Construction of Transnational Justice* (Routledge 2012); Sara Dezalay, 'Weakness as Routine in the Operations of the Intentional Criminal Court' 17 International Criminal Law Review 281.

make the social structure of this space analytically intelligible. This is crucial to understand since the individuals working in the distinct social fields are likely not only to rely on distinct rulesets, but also to interpret common rules and norms of very differently. To study transnational criminal justice, instead of just its laws, necessitates a perspective that can catch how stakeholders use this law and to what end. In doing so, the article will study how these spaces are structured socially and whether they can be conceived as belonging to the same field of practice.

Previous scholarship has also relied on social science perspectives to analyse the systemic character of new transnational legal phenomena. World systems theory has been used to study global megastructures, including internationalised forms of criminal law.[27] Similar perspectives have been used to analyse transnational anti-corruption law in action[28] that draws upon the systems theory of Günther Teubner's 'regimes'[29] and Gregory Shaffer's idea of transnational 'legal orders',[30] ultimately preferring the latter to conceptualise the practices of the studied form of law. This concept allows for an investigation of how transnational norms affect national jurisdictions, but, from the vantage point of a Bourdieu inspired analysis, overlooks the importance of the social conditions under which these norms are created and that guide their perspectives and implementation. Transnational crime has also attracted the attention of internationally oriented sociologists, although these scholars have studied specific forms of criminal law beyond the state rather than investigated its systematic characteristics.[31] These studies generally target precisely transnational fields, networks and practices and thus focus on both international and regional developments.[32] Another common thread of this scholarship is that it turns its attention not to the criminal activity sought controlled by legal and law enforcement means, but to the development of justice and policing practices developed to suppress transnational crime. All of the four transnational sectors of criminal law studied in this article have been the object of attention

27 Lechner and Boli 215.

28 Kevin E. Davis, Guillermo Jorge and Maíra R. Machado, 'Transnational Anticorruption Law in Action: Cases from Argentina and Brazil' 40 Law & Social Inquiry 664.

29 Gunther Teubner and Peter Korth, 'Two kinds of legal pluralism: Collision of transnational regimes in the double fragmentation of world society'.

30 Gregory C. Shaffer, *Transnational Legal Ordering and State Change* (9781139206662, Cambridge University Press 2012).

31 Monique Nuijten and Gerhard Anders (eds), *Corruption and the Secret of Law: A Legal Anthropological Perspective* (075467682X, Ashgate 2007); James Sheptycki, 'Critical reflections on transnational crime and transnational police' 47 Criminologie 13.

32 Didier Bigo, *Mapping the Field of EU Internal Security Agencies* (L'Harmattan 2007).

from this scholarship. Drug trafficking, for instance, has spurred a significant social science literature.[33] So has the domain of anti-terrorism, especially over the past two decades, where sociologists have focused on how new police and security initiatives were initiated to curb the new form of international terrorism,[34] the terminology of the field also being deployed to show how counter-terrorism helped entrench specific developments in the European field of security conceptualised here as a social space that cuts across specific legal domains.[35] Other sociologists have investigated law enforcement practices that target drug trafficking[36] or other global phenomena related to policing practices,[37] as well as the workings of the fight against environmental crime[38] or anti-corruption.[39] International practices of prosecution more broadly have also been investigated with a focus on the export of national law enforcement perspectives to other countries[40] and the conflict between national bureaucracies and international prosecution.[41] While these studies have investigated

---

33 Jörg Friedrichs, *Fighting Terrorism and Drugs: Europe and International Police Cooperation* (Routledge 2008); Ethan A. Nadelmann, 'Global prohibition regimes: the evolution of norms in international society' 44 International Organization 479.

34 Mathieu Deflem, *The policing of terrorism: Organizational and global perspectives* (Routledge 2010); Mathieu Deflem, 'Social Control and the Policing of Terrorism: Foundations for a Sociology of Counterterrorism' 35 American Sociologist 75.

35 Didier Bigo, 'Globalized (in)security: The field and the ban-opticon' in Didier Bigo and Anastassia Tsoukala (eds), *Terror, Insecurity and Liberty: Illiberal practices of liberal regimes after 9/11* (Routledge 2008); Laurent Bonelli, Didier Bigo and Thomas Deltombe, 'Au nom du 11 septembre. Les démocraties occidentales à l'épreuve de l'antiterrorisme'.

36 Benjamin Bowling, *Policing the Caribbean: Transnational Security Cooperation in Practice* (Oxford University Press 2010).

37 Benjamin Bowling and J.W.E. Sheptycki, *Global policing* (Los Angeles, Calif.; London: SAGE 2012); J.W.E. Sheptycki (ed), *Issues in Transnational Policing* (Routledge 2000); Markus Dirk Dubber, *The new police science, the police power in domestic and international governance* (080475392X, Stanford University Press 2006); Ron Levi and John Hagan, 'International Police' in Markus D Dubber and Mariana Valverde (eds), *The New Police Science: The Police Power in Domestic and International Govenance* (Stanford University Press 2006).

38 Rob White, *Transnational environmental crime: Toward an eco-global criminology* (Routledge 2011).

39 Pierre Lascoumes, 'Change and Resistance in the Fight Against Corruption' 19 French politics, culture, and society 49 Davis, Jorge and Machado.

40 Ethan Avram Nadelmann, *Cops across borders, the internationalization of U.S. criminal law enforcement* (0271010940, Pennsylvania State University Press 1993).

41 Mikkel Jarle Christensen, 'International Prosecution and National Bureaucracy: The Contest to Define International Practices within the Danish Prosecution Service' Law & Social Inquiry.

links between different legal spaces of enforcement mechanisms and their relation to specific fields of practice, they have not attempted to grasp the larger structures of transnational criminal justice.

To conduct what is, admittedly, an exploratory analysis of precisely how international criminal justice is organised as a social space (or more precisely as several interrelated social spaces), the article builds on original empirical material. As the core of this material 89 career trajectories have been gathered from counter-terrorism, anti-corruption, environmental crime fighting and drug crime enforcement. While this limited sample obviously does not provide the basis of a comprehensive study of these domains and the contest to define, for instance, anti-corruption,[42] it aims to provide an emblematic section of the elites engaged in the investigated sectors. To secure a sampling of profiles that are not atypical to the spaces of practice in question, the 89 profiles have been collected from organisations involved in arranging the major conference events in the four sectors. The underlying assumption is that the profiles involved in these events are exemplary for the wider structure of the space in question, or at least not completely alien to it as they have been able to secure prominent positions within it. The profiles used for the explorative analysis of the social structure of transnational criminal justice were drawn from the advisory and planning boards of the International Drug Enforcement Conference (IDEC), the International Conference on Counter-Terrorism, the International Conference on Environmental Crime and the International Anti-Corruption Conference. In the case of IDEC, initiated in 1983 by the American Drug Enforcement Administration (DEA) that also maintains control over and co-finances the events, other agents involved have been included in the material, concretely the Community Anti-Drug Coalitions of America (CADCA) that works closely with the DEA, the Commission on Narcotic Drugs (CND) and the International Narcotics Control Board (INCB). In addition to this material, the article draws more generally on more than 150 interviews of professionals engaged in international and transnational criminal justice. As indicated by DEA control with the IDEC, the analysis of career characteristics is not only of interest as a professional phenomenon. At a deeper structural level, investigating the internal organisation of these spaces, focusing on their social balances and the forms of professional, symbolic and financial capital invested in them, reveals their diachronic development and the power balances that

42 Mikkel Jarle Christensen, 'Crafting and Promoting International Crimes: A Controversy between Legal Professionals of Core Crimes and Anti-Corruption' *Leiden Journal of International Law*.

shape interactions within them, including the crafting and interpretation of the relevant legal mechanisms and technologies.

II From International to Transnational Criminal Law and Justice

The conceptual distinction between international and transnational criminal law was fine-tuned in the wake of the massive political and legal investments into the former during the 1990s. In the decades before the institution building that began with the creation of the International Criminal Tribunal for the former Yugoslavia (ICTY), international criminal law was generally understood to cover all types of internationally codified crime, although it made a distinction between international criminal law *strictu sensu*, and crimes of international concern.[43] What separated these two subgenres of crime in Bassiouni's system was that international crimes were enforceable in international criminal tribunals based on individual criminal responsibility, while crimes of international concern were codified in international conventions but enforceable by national systems. However, with the development of a more distinct field of practice around the crimes of genocide, crimes against humanity and war crimes, driven by the creation of new international criminal courts and the creation of a new social, political and legal economy around them, this space also began policing its boundaries with respect to what forms of crime could be seen as international criminal law. This field of practice has enjoyed massive academic interest from legal scholars as well as from social scientists.[44] On the contrary, other forms of crime have not enjoyed the same interest. The conceptualisation of TCL as a form of legal space is an attempt to reimagine the treaty based crimes that were left out of international criminal law[45] and in the process re-legitimise them as an object worthy of scholarly interest.[46] In a broader context, the recalibration of scholarly interest towards TCL also aims to identify deficiencies in previous understandings of the many treaties systematised under this domain and thus also point to possible solutions, by crafting clear legal and procedural principles for this form of law.

43 M. Cherif Bassiouni, *International Criminal Law* (Transnational Publishers 1986).

44 van Sliedregt Sergey Vasiliev, 'On Trajectories and Destinations of International Criminal Law Scholarship' 28 *Leiden Journal of International Law* 701.

45 Boister, 'The Exclusion of Treaty Crimes from the Jurisdiction of the Proposed International Criminal Court: Law, Pragmatism, Politics'.

46 Robert J. Currie, *An Introduction to Transnational Criminal Law.* (*Book review*) (2015).

TCL is theoretically seen as distinct system because of its indirect nature that stands in contrast to the direct nature of ICL. Transnational crimes also stand apart from international crimes by being conducted mainly by private actors, while international criminal law deal with state conduct and established individual criminal responsibility directly under international law.[47] As such, TCL has only limited scope for extraterritorial jurisdiction in contrast to the self-proclaimed universality of ICL. These distinctions, however, presuppose the existence of a distinct domain of ICL against which TCL can be defined. However, stakeholders are continuously trying to renegotiate the boundaries of these two legal domains at a practical as well as a theoretical level. For instance, ICL is under constant renegotiation from national, regional and other stakeholders who attempt to redirect this form of law in the direction of other crimes, often precisely the crimes systematised under the heading of TCL. As such, all of the sectors investigated in this article have been the subject of drives to include them under the umbrella of ICL or more concretely under the subject-matter jurisdiction of the ICC. Scholars as well as NGO advocates—keeping in mind that these two groups are often overlapping or work for the same ends—have promoted the expansion of ICL to include terrorism,[48] drug trafficking,[49] environmental crimes[50] and corruption.[51] However, it should be noted that all of these initiatives have been met with criticism from scholars as well as practitioners[52] and have remained marginal irritants in the borderlands around ICL. Nonetheless, the two spaces are linked if not practically in the daily lives of international criminal courts and as national systems face both types of crimes then through the promotion of new international crimes. Such promotional strategies often aim to

---

47 Claus Kreß, *International Criminal Law* (2009).

48 Roberta Arnold, *The ICC as a New Instrument for Repressing Terrorism* (Ardsley, N.Y.: Transnational Publishers 2004).

49 Juan Carlos Sainz-Borgo, 'The International Criminal Court, Drug Trafficking and Crimes Against Humanity: A Local Interpretation of the Rome Statute' 15 *The Journal Jurisprudence* 373.

50 Steven Freeland, *Addressing the Intentional Destruction of the Environment during Warfare under the Rome Statute of the International Criminal Court* (Interstitia Ltd 2015); Jacqueline Hellman, 'The Fifth Crime Under International Criminal Law: Ecocide?' in Dominik Brodowski and others (eds), *Regulating Corporate Criminal Liability* (Springer International Publishing 2014) <http://dx.doi.org/10.1007/978-3-319-05993-8_22>.

51 Mark L. Wolf, 'The Case for an International Anti-Corruption Court' (Washington, DC) [Brookings Institute] Governance Studies at Brookings.

52 Christensen, 'Crafting and Promoting International Crimes: A Controversy between Legal Professionals of Core Crimes and Anti-Corruption'.

circumvent the dominance of states in the space of TCL by imbuing it with the institutional resources active in ICL.[53]

Neil Boister has contributed the core theoretical claim of TCL scholarship. At the core of this claim is the idea that TCL exists as a distinct legal and political 'system'[54] composed of more than 200 legal instruments. This system is seen to have two main functions in aiming 1) to suppress transnational crime and 2) to transnationalise criminal law through the diffusion of legal technologies and practices. In this context, building on Jessup's concept of transnational law,[55] TCL becomes the doctrinal equivalent to the more well-established concept of transnational crime used in social science, particularly criminology.[56] Building on earlier contributions,[57] the concept of transnational criminal law crafted by Boister constructs a dualistic model that signifies: "the indirect suppression by international law through domestic penal law of criminal activities that have actual or potential trans-boundary effects".[58] In the present volume, Boister shows TCL in fact creates a "fictional transnational legal space" in which specific stakeholders, often technocrats, operate. These technocrats are also involved in policy building which is the object of this article.

The push to reimagine TCL comes from specific parts of the academic field oriented towards trans-border crimes and law. American law and society scholars have mainly been preoccupied with national security or policy issues and their relation to transnational crime dynamics,[59] with testing the US scholarly debates on international objects[60] or with local case studies of crime enforce-

---

53 Neil Boister, 'International Tribunals for Transnational Crimes: Towards a Transnational Criminal Court?' (Dordrecht) 23 Criminal Law Forum 295.

54 Boister, *An Introduction to Transnational Criminal Law* 13.

55 Philip Jessup, *Transnational law* (Yale University Press 1956).

56 Boister, 'Transnational Criminal Law?' 953.

57 Albin Eser and Otto Lagodny, *Principles and Procedures for a New Transnational Criminal Law* (3922498639, Max-Planck-Institut 1992).

58 Boister, 'Transnational Criminal Law?' 955.

59 Neve Gordon, 'Human Rights as a Security Threat: Lawfare and the Campaign against Human Rights NGOs' 48 Law & Society Review 311; Katherine Beckett and Heather Evans, 'Crimmigration at the Local Level: Criminal Justice Processes in the Shadow of Deportation' 49 Law & Society Review 241; Elizabeth Chiarello, 'The War on Drugs Comes to the Pharmacy Counter: Frontline Work in the Shadow of Discrepant Institutional Logics' 40 Law & Social Inquiry 86.

60 John Hagan, Joshua Kaiser and Anna Hanson, *Iraq and the Crimes of Aggressive War, The Legal Cynicism of Criminal Militarism* (9781316221693, Cambridge University Press 2015).

ment in other countries.[61] European social scientists have focused primarily on the emergence of a regional space of criminal law and justice often tied to the European Union (EU).[62] Similar fault lines can be seen in legal scholarship that has focused, for instance, on European regional transnationalism.[63] The focus on TCL as a new legal system stems mainly from outside of these scholarly circles, geographically from countries outside Northern Europe and the US. However, they stem from closely linked English speaking academic markets with particular interests in transnational crime, such as New Zealand, Australia and Canada or from professional economies historically linked to larger European markets, but also placed at their periphery, such as Singapore.[64] The concept of TCL underlines linkages that are evident in countries closely affiliated with world economy and its scientific hubs, but located at its periphery in terms of their geographical placement and role in the wider system of transnational criminal law. Scholarly investments in TCL is a way to couple local academic and political perceptions to international research and policy development, pointing to the interconnectedness of crime across borders and thus to the need for systematisation and conceptualisation of the law that governs these transversal practices. The concept of TCL insists on the existence of a larger system and thus attempts to place a new research new agenda in the scholarly mainstream by demonstrating the importance of their object and the impact of the identified types of crime and lacking understanding of the legal mechanisms set up to control them. Of course, the concept of transnational criminal law is not the exclusive domain of scholars placed outside of the US or Europe.[65] However, while the highly sophisticated

---

61 John Braithwaite and Ali Gohar, 'Restorative Justice, Policing and Insurgency: Learning from Pakistan' 48 Law & Society Review 531.

62 Didier Bigo, *Europe's 21st Century Challenge: Delivering Liberty* (Ashgate Pub. Co. 2010); Bigo, *Mapping the Field of EU Internal Security Agencies*; Elspeth Guild, Sergio Carrera and Thierry Balzacq, 'The Changing Dynamics of Security in an Enlarged European Union' in Didier Bigo and others (eds), *Europe's 21st Century Challenge: Delivering Liberty* (Ashgate 2010).

63 Valsamis Mitsilegas, *EU Criminal Law* (Hart Publishing 2009); André Klip, *European criminal law, an integrative approach* (1780680015, Intersentia 2012).

64 Wui Ling Cheah, 'Fair treatment in transnational and international criminal law' 25 *Singapore Academy of Law Journal* 778.

65 Sabine Gless, 'Bird's-eye view and worm's-eye view: towards a defendant-based approach in transnational criminal law' [Routledge] 6 Transnational Legal Theory 117; Sabine Gless and John A.E. Vervaele, 'Editorial
Law Should Govern: Aspiring General Principles for Transnational Criminal Justice' 9 Utrecht Law Review 1; David Luban, Julie R. O'Sullivan and David P. Stewart, *International and transnational criminal law* (Second edition.

systematisation built around TCL has gained some footing in academic discourse it competes with other scholarly agendas that conceptualise transnational practices of justice in different ways more closely related to regional, national and popular understandings of crime patterns. In this contest, TCL competes not only with ICL for attention and, presumably, funding, but also with scholarly investments in transnational practices that are defined less by their perception of a global system and more by their focus on specific crimes of regional or national interest. In a sense, the conceptualisation becomes part of the wider space of transnational criminal justice initiatives that are the object of the present article.

III The Social Structure of Transnational Criminal Justice

While the skilful crafting of TCL as a theoretical endeavour has created an intellectual framework around which scholars, policy builders and practitioners can reconceive their strategies and ideals, the social dynamics that govern this structure and the rules of the game played there must be studied as an empirical sociological phenomenon. It must be studied more broadly as justice initiatives rather as merely interpretation of the law. The investigation of the wider social space that drives TCL also reopens the conceptual question of what type of a criminal justice domain can be said to exist beyond the state and outside of the international criminal courts. More concretely it opens the question if what is labelled a 'system' by Boister is in fact four separate spaces tied to two specific social fields of practice in the definition of Pierre Bourdieu and what impact this has on the structuration of practices and ideologies in this larger space. This is not merely of theoretical interest, but is crucial for understanding how TCL actually works and which social, political and legal forces drive its development. The analysis will proceed in four sections that analyse each of the chosen legal sectors (or spaces) oriented towards drug trafficking, terrorism, corruption and environmental crimes. The investigation of each of these sectors will focus on the structural and social composition of these spaces and will also be related to other sociological analyses of this particular phenomenon. While the individual sections investigate social composition within this

---

edn, Wolters Kluwer Law & Business 2014); Roger Cotterrell, 'The Concept of Crime and Transnational Networks of Community' in Valsamis Mitsilegas, Peter Aldridge and Leonidas Cheliotis (eds), *Globalisation, Criminal Law and Criminal Justice: Theoretical, Comparative and Transnational Perspectives* (Hart 2014).

space, it will consider in particular for linkages to other spaces to assess the overall social structure of transnational criminal justice.

1 *Drug Trafficking*

From the late 1960s the fight against drug trafficking, or the war on drugs as then US President Nixon labelled it in a 1971 speech, has become a core practice in most police forces and criminal justice systems. That a US President was behind the coinage of the phrase that would come to epitomise transnational responses to drugs was not coincidental. The American Drug Enforcement Administration (DEA) was very active in exporting a zero-tolerance to drugs to other jurisdictions.[66] The DEA was created in 1973, taking over an organisation that had roots in the prohibition movement. It grew rapidly. The agency currently has a budget of 2.03 billion dollars (a number that has decreased during the financial crunch, from 2.4 billion in 2008) and employs close to 5,000 special agents.[67] Backed by massive resources, the consequences of US drug policies in South America, particularly in Colombia,[68] also well-known from popular media, have been well established. Feeding the imaginary of why fighting drugs is a security concern, scholars have also pointed to the linkages between drug trafficking and terrorism in this region.[69] The effects of the American war on drugs had much wider effects on transnational law enforcement.[70] In a country such as Denmark, usually known alongside its Scandinavian neighbours for its lenient criminal justice policy that mixed repressive and liberal elements,[71] the DEA actively helped reshape police practices through training of Danish officers and by lending large cash amounts to the police of Copenhagen to use for sting operations against what was believed to be a highly organised

66 Ethan Avram Nadelmann, *Cops across borders: the internationalization of U.S. criminal law enforcement* (Pennsylvania State University Press 1993).

67 DEA website visited 1.11.2016.

68 Winifred Tate, *Drugs, Thugs, and Diplomats U.S. Policymaking in Colombia* (9780804795678, Stanford University Press 2015).

69 Laura Garces, 'Colombia: The Link between Drugs and Terror' 35 *Journal of Drug Issues* 83; Tobias Franz, 'Plan Colombia: illegal drugs, economic development and counterinsurgency—a political economy analysis of Colombia's failed war' 34 Development Policy Review 563.

70 J.W.E. Sheptycki, *Law Enforcement, Justice and Democracy in the Transnational Arena: Reflections on the War on Drugs* (1996).

71 Tapio Lappi-Seppälä, 'Penal Policies in the Nordic Countries 1960–2010' [Taylor & Francis Group] 13 *Journal of Scandinavian Studies in Criminology and Crime Prevention* 85.

network of drug traffickers.[72] Specialised units for policing drugs were created throughout much of the world and became a significant part of the daily work of police departments.

As previously mentioned, the main international conference on criminal justice responses to drugs, the International Drug Enforcement Conference (IDEC), was created in 1983 by the DEA, which also co-funds the annual conference in collaboration with the host nation. Participants are mainly heads of national police forces or of specialised domestic units dealing with drug control. Other stakeholders include the UN Office on Drugs and Crime (UNODC) that assists the International Drug Control Board (INCB) and the Commission on Narcotic Drugs (CND) in their treaty based functions under the 1961 Single Convention on Narcotic Drugs, the Convention on Psychotropic Substances of 1971, and the United Nations Convention against Illicit Traffic in Narcotic Drugs and Psychotropic Substances of 1988. The CND functions as the governing body of UNODC and is headed by a UN-style board of rotating ambassadors from different countries and the UNODC is currently managed by the former Russian diplomat and deputy Foreign Minister, Yury Fedotov. The INCB was established by the Single Convention and is an independent and quasi-judicial expert body with 13 members, ten of whom are chosen by UN and non-UN states and the last three by the World Health Organization (WHO). The head of the INCB, German lawyer Werner Sipp, has extensive experience in drug control from the national as well as international context and thus embodies the perception of the fight against drugs that has been institutionalised at both levels since the 1970s.

Despite calls to inscribe drug trafficking into the subject matter jurisdiction of an international criminal court, drug enforcement has remained transnational and is institutionalised mainly in national police forces and criminal justice systems. As was the case in Copenhagen, highly specialised drug enforcement units have become embedded in the structure of these systems in which they deal with a crime area that has high priority in most states. In other words in this specific domain, transnational cooperation is highly routinised in specific offices for which working along national lines is considered essential and who are simultaneously situated close to state power where they exercise significant discretion in the quest to wage war on drugs. At the transnational level of organising knowledge sharing and creating networks that can be used operatively in concrete drug cases, this social and professional structuration is also obvious. National representatives dominate the planning

72 Christensen, 'International Prosecution and National Bureaucracy: The Contest to Define International Practices within the Danish Prosecution Service'.

and coordination of conferences and knowledge production, and although international organisations are also involved, their engagement largely mirrors that of the nation states they represent, something that is evident in the CND's oversight with the UNODC and in the leadership of the latter.

The national and criminal justice founded structuration of the battle against drugs is also evident in NGO involvement. The world's largest anti-drug coalition, CADCA, founded in 1992, has the mission of "building drug-free communities", drug-free here meaning only drugs certified by the medicinal industry that helps fund the coalition. This organisation is of interest here because it works closely with the DEA and provides a central part of the social map of drug trafficking stakeholders. CADCA is based in the US and led by a board that consists of business profiles, former politicians and military personnel—the president and CEO, Arthur T. Dean, retiring from the US Army in 1998 at the rank of Major General. The organisation is financed through grants and contracts, and also receives significant funds from the medicinal industry, the largest partners in 2015 being Johnson & Johnson, Mallinckrodt Pharmaceuticals and McNeil Consumer Healthcare.[73] CADCA works primarily in the US and the Americas where they champion a drug-free communities, help organise local NGOs and perform training sessions for local anti-drug advocates. In the EU, Europe Against Drugs (EURAD) was established in 1989 by the European Commission that also supplies the main funding for this organisation that advocates prevention and treatment. Compared to CADCA, EURAD has a less staunch perspective on ridding society of drugs and focuses instead on alleviating the social and individual costs of drug abuse. The EU has also funded initiatives that try to fuse anti-drugs initiatives with anti-corruption. The *CRIMJUST* project begun in 2016 was built in cooperation between the UNODC, Interpol and Transparency International and aims to strengthen the coordination of efforts along the cocaine route that runs through Latin America, the Caribbean and West Africa.

The social space of drug enforcement is dominated by American influence and driven by the role of the DEA that actively transnationalised their perspectives and practices in the 1960s. While the war on drugs has come under increasing academic and popular criticism in recent years,[74] and some countries and states have, for instance, liberalised access to marijuana or begun treatment of addicts with heroin. However, these initiatives are still peripheral to the main practices that operate the transnational perspective on drug abuse. Using the

73 CADCA, *CADCA Annual Report 2015* (2016) 23.

74 Paula Mallea, *The War on Drugs, A Failed Experiment* (Dundurn 2014); Alan Marzilli and David L. Hudson, *The War on Drugs* (Infobase Publishing 2011).

ideal type developed by Herbert Packer, the enforcement perspective on drugs follows the crime control model[75] and is based on repression. The space of stakeholders around drugs is characterised by the gravitational pull exerted by this model both in terms of ideology and of the bureaucracies in which it is embedded and from where it is reproduced at a transnational level. Adding to this gravitational pull is the involvement of the pharmaceutical industry that supports anti-drugs policies supported by law enforcement. By connecting these policies to medical expertise, these companies and the activities they fund provide an extra layer of legitimacy to the ideological orthodoxy of this space based on a tough stance on illegal drugs based on policing practices on one hand and big business on the other.

2 *Terrorism*

At an international level, the relationship between criminal law and terrorism has a long history. In 1937, an international treaty established the first international criminal court to adjudicate criminal responsibility precisely for international terrorism, but the treaty was never implemented.[76] Fifty years later, during perestroika, the USSR suggested the creation of an international criminal court again to deal with terrorism.[77] While Gorbachev's 1987 suggestion did not gain traction, it helped open the geopolitical space in which Trinidad and Tobago's 1989 call for an international anti-drug court would situate itself. As these proposals demonstrate, international terrorism has been raised as a concern in different waves and mainly been considered a problem at an international and transnational level when it occurred in the Global North. The wave of terrorism in Western Europe during the 1960s and 1970s gave rise to numerous regional initiatives some of which were organised under the TREVI network created in 1975, partly in response to the hostage taking during the 1972 Olympics in Munich where 11 Israeli athletes were killed.[78] While terrorism has been a driver in European integration under what later became known as the Area of Justice and Home Affairs (JHA), the transnational cooperation between European countries also came to include a number of other areas on which the EU's units for police and prosecutorial collaboration, Europol and

75 Herbert L. Packer, 'Two Models of the Criminal Process' [The University of Pennsylvania Law Review] 113 University of Pennsylvania Law Review 1.

76 Mark Lewis, *The Birth of the New Justice: The Internationalization of Crime and Punishment, 1919–1950* (Oxford University Press 2014) 133.

77 Mikhail Gorbachev, *Realities and Guarantees for a Secure World* (Novosti Press Agency Publishing House 1987) 10.

78 Tony Bunyan, 'Trevi, Europol and the European state' Statewatching the new Europe 1.

Eurojust, would also work. These units were also active in defining European approaches to the new wave of terrorism that had 9/11 as its most monumental manifestation.[79]

Despite the intense international attention paid towards terrorism the main enforcement, responses remained national in character. In a broader perspective, the problem and problematisation of international terrorism was tied to a fairly narrow ecology of stakeholders. The International Institute for Counter-Terrorism (ICT), one of the leading in this sector, organises annual world summits on this crime. Founded in 1996 by former Israeli politicians, military commanders of the Israeli Defence Force (IDF), national intelligence agencies and senior members of the Mossad, the ICT is an independent think tank that brings together scholars, practitioners and the security industry to discuss counter-terrorism. The professional advisory board includes individuals with a strong profile in the security industry associated, for instance, with the large French multinational firm the Thales Group, and representatives from smaller firms, which offer consultancy services in the domain of counter terrorism. The nationality of the board is heavily skewed towards Israel and the US and includes only one member from a non-Western country: Rohan Gunaratha, head of the International Centre for Political Violence and Terrorism Research, Singapore, a country that has been a close ally in the US led war on terror. The board is also extremely male-dominated, also in comparison to the other spaces analysed in this article, and counts only one female, Pauline Neville-Jones, Former Minister of State for Security and Counter-Terrorism in the United Kingdom. Of course, the ICT is far from the only think tank that has performed research and consults on terrorism and the last decades have seen a significant proliferation of counter-terrorism expertise, often located precisely at the crossroads between academia, policy development and practice, a mix also seen in career trajectories in this space. In the context of the US, several think tanks have also devoted resources specifically to counter-terrorism, including the Cato Institute, Brookings Institute and the RAND Cooperation.

The strong dominance of Western countries in the definition of terrorism is evident also outside individual organisations. The online international journal, *Perspectives on Terrorism*, has identified 110 terrorism research centres.[80] Sixty-two were located in the US or were partnered with American institutions.

---

79 Bigo, 'Globalized (in)security: The field and the ban-opticon' Didier Bigo, 'Delivering Liberty and Security? The Reframing of Freedom when Associated with Security' in Didier Bigo and others (eds), *Europe's 21st Century Challenge: Delivering Liberty* (Ashgate 2010).

80 Benjamin Freedman, 'Terrorism Research Centres' 4 Perspectives on Terrorism.

The other centres were typically located in the Global North or in countries that related to the geopolitical interests of the West, 12 in Western Europe or Australia and the remainder in countries such as Israel, Singapore, Egypt, India and Bangladesh, one centre being located in China. While this list may also suffer from a Western-oriented bias and must be understood in relation to the relative strength of professional markets and its funding bodies, it is clear that the substantial intellectual and material resources being invested into counter-terrorism flow from a very particular part of the world. This does not mean that there are not differences of opinion among the many organisations involved in counter-terrorism. However, these differences are organised intellectually within the same common understanding of the need to create effective counter-terrorism measures and defend especially Western societies against what is most often perceived as an external enemy. The stakeholders involved share important professional traits and the main forms of capital active in this space are located at the borderline between policing, military and commercial interests.

At an operative level, counter-terrorism is situated at the border between the police and the military. Europol and Interpol coordinate efforts against terrorism and the bulk of this work falls under the purview of national intelligence agencies, most often those controlled by the police. In other words, the power relations between the police and the military, during the Cold War being dominated by the latter (Bigo 1993), have shifted in favour of the former.[81] These intelligence agencies played a significant, but often quite discreet, role in defining the new terrorism that emerged after 2001 in effect accelerating the development of a new set of bureaucratically embedded practices that predated the terror attacks in New York and Washington.[82] While the particular national response to the new terror was characterised by specific historical understandings of political violence—UK experiences with Northern Ireland being different from Germany's history, for instance—as well as impacted by the palace wars between different ministries and other parts of the public system, in most Western states intelligence agencies regrouped around the notion of Islamic terrorism that gave them new legitimacy and often opened the path to more funding.

---

81 Didier Bigo, 'When two become one' in Morten Kelstrup and Michael Charles Williams (eds), *International relations theory and the politics of European integration: Power, security, and community* (Routledge 2000).

82 Laurent Bonelli, '"Hidden in plain sight": Intelligence, exception and suspicion after 11 September 2001' in Didier Bigo and Anastassia Tsoukala (eds), *Terror, Insecurity and Liberty: Illiberal practices of liberal regimes after 9/11* (Routledge 2008).

The social structure of counter-terrorism is characterised by a structural transformation that begun in the aftermath of the Cold War but was accelerated by the emergence of new terrorist threats. Regional and international cooperation was crucial in the definition of this threat and in policy development of Western governments. In the definition of a new security landscape, intelligence agencies and what Didier Bigo calls police 'guilds',[83] coexisted with scholars who offered their intellectual and sometimes practical expertise to governments and think tanks. These organisations brought together stakeholders who laid bare the rest of the social space in which terrorism was defined and counter-terrorism initiatives outlined. In this space, international companies built on developing concrete security solutions were also active and capitalised on the emergence of new threats. While no globally accepted legal definition of terrorism exists,[84] the Western security agencies, scholars/ policy advocates and companies that dominate this social space share a common perspective on some of the main forms of terrorism of the past decades. The differences between terror lists should not subtract from the fact that the gravity of this social space is organised around a specific perspective on terrorism that constantly produces and reproduces common yet esoteric transnational perceptions. This perspective is embedded institutionally in the many law enforcement initiatives crafted around terrorism that are closely related to state power, especially through national intelligence agencies.

3 *Corruption*

Global anti-corruption initiatives are of a later date than both the war on drugs or counter-terrorism. Among the earliest practices in this still emerging sector were US legislation crafted in the wake of the Watergate scandal. The 1977 Foreign Corrupt Practices Act forbids American companies from bribing public officials of other nations. While new initiatives on money laundering were created in the 1980s in parallel to Reagan's continuation of the war on drugs, it was not until the 1990s that more transnational norms of anti-corruption

83 Didier Bigo, 'The transnational field of computerised exchange of information in police matters and its European guilds' in Niilo Kauppi and Mikael Rask Madsen (eds), *Transnational Power Elites: The new professionals of governance, law and security* (Routledge 2013).

84 Eva Herschinger, 'A Battlefield of Meanings: The Struggle for Identity in the UN Debates on a Definition of International Terrorism' [Taylor & Francis Group] 25 Terrorism and Political Violence 183.

began to emerge and influence national legal systems.[85] In 1994, European Ministers of Justice agreed to work towards a joint regional strategy to combat corruption. This decision gave impetus to the formation of the 1999 GRECO group on corruption as well as two CoE conventions opened for signature in 1999. Outside of government control, a central component in the anti-corruption movement was the creation of Transparency International (TI) in 1993.[86] This NGO was founded by Peter Eigen, formerly a high ranking employee in the World Bank, alongside a group of legal professionals, including scholars and practitioners, and journalists. Based on close contacts to governments and international organisations, TI adopted practices aimed at measuring and comparing the perception of corruption in different countries. Their annual Corruption Perception Index aims, besides providing an international benchmark of anti-corruption, to be a tool that will stimulate compliance with anti-corruption norms.

The social space of transnational anti-corruption being originally founded on notions of compliance, strategies of prosecution have not until recently impacted this sector and it remains divided between proponents of criminal law approaches and stakeholders more engaged with consultancy work and cooperation with states and companies. A number of international anti-corruption initiatives have been created since the 1990s, such as the 1994 OECD Anti-bribery convention which was part of a broader effort in this organisation to combat corruption, the 1999 Council of Europe (CoE) Criminal Law Convention on Corruption, and the 2003 UN Convention Against Corruption (UNCAC). Most of these initiatives build on soft law norms and are enforceable through national jurisdictions. Around these initiatives, a social space of "integrity warriors" has emerged.[87] These warriors are based in international NGOs of which TI remained the most prolific and in national jurisdictions where they

85 Cecily Rose, *International Anti-Corruption Norms. Their Creation and Influence on Domestic Legal Systems* (Oxford University Press 2015); Cecily Rose, *Corruption: A Violation of Human Rights and a Crime under International Law?* (2014).

86 Ellen Gutterman, 'The Legitimacy of Transnational NGOs: Lessons from the Experience of Transparency International in Germany and France' (London) 40 Review of International Studies 391.

87 Luís de Sousa, Peter Larmour and Barry Hindess (eds), *Governments, NGOs and Anti-Corruption: The New Integrity Warriors* (0415466954, Routledge 2009); Steven Sampson, 'Integrity warriors: global morality and the anti-corruption movement in the Balkans' Corruption: anthropological perspectives 103.

work in specialised anti-corruption units. As these sprung up across the world, a veritable "anti-corruption industry" was created.[88]

The International Anti-Corruption Conference (IACC) is one of the largest events in this sector. It is planned jointly by the IACC, TI and its local chapter in the hosting country. The 2014 event brought in around 1200 delegates from some 130 different countries. Unlike in the spaces of drugs and terrorism, the program committee of the IACC is not as evidently dominated by Western professionals. Out of its 13 members, seven are from the Global South (including Argentina, Brazil, Ethiopia, Colombia and Peru), and seven are female. The stakeholders in the IACC represent the wider ecology of this social space characterised by NGO advocacy and government and governance officials without direct access to the coercive tools of national enforcement systems, save for Robert Leventhal, director of the Anticrime programs division, US Department of State. Most other professionals were placed at a more international level where policy development, support and advocacy are the focus. An example was Phil Matsheza, regional cluster leader of the UN Development Programme (UNDP) based in Bangkok, Thailand, whose profile testifies to the engagement of international organisations in anti-corruption measures. Besides TI, the anti-corruption NGO, SHERPA, is represented in the IACC. SHERPA aims to protect and defend victims of economic crimes in the developing world and builds on the expertise of lawyers used also to champion specific ideals of good governance. The mix of legal expertise and advocacy is evident in the many NGOs involved in this space and organised, for instance, in the UNCAC Coalition and slowly pulling the social space of anti-corruption in the direction of criminal law to supplement that of compliance originally created by TI. One example is the Socio-Economic Rights and Accountability Project (SERAP) based in Lagos, Nigeria. SERAP has been very active in bringing litigation to national and international courts brought the SERAP v. Nigeria before the ECOWAS court.[89] The case concerns Nigeria's former first lady who allegedly received "small gifts" amounting to 15 million dollars while her husband was in government. SERAP, supported by the Open Society Foundation (OSF), has also tried to bring cases to the ICC arguing that corruption Nigeria was systemic and widespread to the extent where it met the Rome Statute's definition of 'crimes against humanity'.[90]

88 Steven Sampson, 'The Anti-Corruption Industry: From Movement to Institution' [Taylor & Francis] 11 Global Crime 261.

89 For judgment see ECW/CCJ/JUD/18/12.

90 Petition of SERAP registered as OTP-CR-245/17.

The attempt to use criminal law as a tool to fight corruption reveals a deeper scission that formats the social space of anti-corruption divided between proponents of cooperative practices based on compliance and advocates of criminal law approaches that typically operate at further distance from national governments and large companies.[91] Some criminal law advocates are part of the transnational *Corruption Hunters Network* built around the profile of Eva Joly who prosecuted the *Elf Aquitaine* case in France.[92] The network defines itself in opposition to the anti-corruption industry that they see as at best superfluous in its insistence on cooperation and thus no substitute for actual prosecutions of corrupt practices. Consequently, the core of the network consists of prosecutors who have been deeply involved in controversial anti-corruption cases in their domestic jurisdiction. Based on this criminal law expertise, the transnational network acts as a platform for sharing experience and as a security measure that can mobilise international attention to domestic prosecutions and to the often highly politically and professionally exposed position of the prosecutors at the helm of these cases. The use of criminal law techniques has also been advocated by agents who call for an International Anti-Corruption Court or an extended subject-matter jurisdiction of the ICC. Senior US Judge, Mark Wolf, who was brought into the US administration in the aftermath of the Watergate scandal and has substantial experience from legal cases involving corruption, recently promoted one such proposal.[93] This proposal, however, has yet to gain traction and other proponents of the criminal law approach see it as unrealistic.[94]

Divided between compliance and criminal law technologies, but moving in recent years towards the latter, the social space of anti-corruption is dominated by national interests. Transnational networks and practices, often driven by NGOs, consciously aim to transcend through litigation and create attention and support for national prosecution. Meanwhile big international businesses have invested in anti-corruption measures and employed former profiles of ICL. M. Cherif Bassiouni and Luis Moreno Ocampo were both deeply involved in the crafting of international criminal law at a scholarly and practical level, and were also both hired by Phillip Morris to aid the company in their anti-corruption campaign. The social homophily between anti-corruption and

91 Christensen, 'Crafting and Promoting International Crimes: A Controversy between Legal Professionals of Core Crimes and Anti-Corruption'.

92 Eva Joly, *Justice Under Siege: One Woman's Battle against a European Oil Company* (Citizen 2006).

93 Wolf.

94 Karen Alter and Juliet Sorensen, *Let Nations, Not the World, Prosecute Corruption* (2014).

companies is pronounced in the part of the field focused on compliance, but this proximity usually disappears closer to the axis of criminal law, although companies will solicit criminal law capital to give legitimacy to their practices. While corruption is often mentioned in connection to other forms of transnational crime, most frequently perhaps drug offences and terrorism, socially and professionally the practices of this space are fairly specific and tied professionally to a very narrow set of interests linked to the opposition between corporate interests and NGO advocacy. The perspectives of the latter are typically not hugely influential in the practice of states when it comes to curbing corruption. Only at the periphery of this ecology do you find attempts to fuse practices of anti-corruption with international criminal law or secure more comprehensive transnational criminal justice initiatives.

4 *Environmental Crime*

The social space of environmental crime is even further removed from the sphere of influence embedded in national bureaucracies and criminal justice systems. Much like in the space of anti-corruption, the emergence of this space was closely related to the creation and influence of specific environmental NGOs. While environmental destruction began to be conceived of as criminal after the Second World War, it was not until the 1990s that advocates of the environment and criminal law expertise gained international traction. In 1994 the UN Economic and Social Council (ECOSOC) passed a resolution (resolution 1994/15) on 'The role of criminal law in the protection of the environment', which featured concrete recommendations to member states. Bringing together ideas from the domain of criminal law and environmental protection, this initiative built on a longer trajectory epitomised in the concept of *ecocide* which first appeared in 1970 and was promoted by Arthur Galston, who was at the forefront of identifying and criticising the use of Agent Orange over Vietnam. The term was picked up by legal scholars in the same period UN organs turned their attention towards criminal law as a governance technology also in the space of environmental crimes.[95]

Like the other spaces of criminal law beyond the state, the social ecology of environmental crimes is characterised by a number of different stakeholders. Significantly, law enforcement representatives from international organisations are more numerous than agents from the national jurisdictions, that have access to the crime control system. These professionals include officers from Interpol's environmental crimes program, the UN Environmental

95 Mark Allan Gray, 'The International Crime of Ecocide' 26 Cal W Int'l LJ 215; Anja Gauger and others, 'Ecocide is the Missing 5th Crime against Peace'.

Program (UNEP) and representatives from the emerging crimes unit from UN's Interregional Crime and Justice Research Institute (UNICRI). The fact that environmental crime remains an emerging crime and does not have the institutional embeddedness of for instance drug crime, which has been woven into national institutions and transnational cooperation for decades, is evident not only in the lack of government engagement, but also in the heavy involvement of NGO advocacy who, allied with legal professionals, are active in trying to raise environmental crimes on the agenda. While such social and professional coalitions dominate much of the public debate, the 2012 International Conference for Environmental Crimes held in Italy did have representation from local law enforcement, specifically anti-mafia prosecutors, something that points to national experience with linkages between organised crime and environmental crime[96] and even with problematic mafia engagement in the legitimate green energy sector.[97] Mafia investments also spurred the conceptual innovation of *ecomafia* that designates precisely organised crime activities based on the handling of illegal waste etc. Former employees of the international criminal courts were also active in this space and in the attempt to refocus international criminal law towards environmental crimes.

At a transnational level, one of the most prominent NGOs is *Eradicating Ecocide* headed by UK barrister, Polly Higgins, an organisation that has close ties to anti-climate change activism. This group promotes the recognition of ecocide as an international crime and push for both national, regional and international forms of enforcement.[98] One avenue of these promotional activities includes inscribing ecocide in the Rome Statute and thus making it enforceable at the ICC. Mixing academic capital, experience from international criminal law in The Hague and ecocide advocacy, one strategy has been to publish pieces that might feed directly into diplomatic negotiations about environmental crimes in the ICC.[99] In line with a more general shift towards environmental crimes in some national jurisdictions, the ICC OTP adopted a new policy paper, published in September 2016, on case selection and

96 Reece Walters, *Dirty collar crime and the environment* (Queensland University of Technology 2012).

97 Stefano Caneppele, Michele Riccardi and Priscilla Standridge, 'Green energy and black economy: mafia investments in the wind power sector in Italy' 59 Crime, Law and Social Change 319.

98 Polly Higgins, Damien Short and Nigel South, 'Protecting the planet: a proposal for a law of ecocide' (Dordrecht) 59 Crime, Law and Social Change 251.

99 Polly Higgins, *Eradicating ecocide* (Shepheard Walwyn (Publishers) 2012) Freeland.

prioritisation.[100] In what many commentators have seen as a change of policy, paragraph 41 of the paper highlights precisely the importance of pursuing environmental crimes, illegal exploitation of natural resources or the illegal dispossession of land. This policy change reflects not only an increased attention towards this form of crime, but also an OTP that has continuously been under attack in recent years, particularly from African states,[101] and has tried to change its strategies to include more easy to prosecute cases such as reflected in the recent conviction of Mr. Al Mahdi for the destruction of buildings of cultural and historical importance in the city of Timbuktu, Mali.[102]

The campaign to make ecocide the fifth international crime alongside genocide, crimes against humanity, war crimes and aggression has roots in the post-WWII era but has yet to have substantive impact although recent developments in the ICC might be seen a break-through for the efforts to raise awareness for this crime. However, in terms of institutional and professional embeddedness, environmental crimes divisions around the world are far from as active and established as those dealing with terrorism, drug trafficking and even those that target corruption. Mirrored also in the social ecology of the space of environmental protection, this crime is primarily championed by NGOs and agents at the periphery of state power.

IV The Structure and Effects of the Four Spaces of Practice

The four different social spaces briefly analysed above, exhibit several differences that affect their social gravity and ideology as well as formatting the practices and strategies of its agents. These differences can be conceptualised through three axes related to state, corporate and geopolitical power that are embodied in the stakeholders of these spaces and their social and professional capital. The first axis is related to the bureaucratic embeddedness of crime fighting initiatives, a close proximity to state power characterising one spectrum of activities—most significantly in relation to drug trafficking and terrorism—and a lower degree of access to this power structuring the strategies of anti-corruption and environmental crime activists and practitioners. The strategies of the professionals involved in these spaces are often directed

100 OTP Office of the Prosecutor, *Policy Paper on Case Selection and Prioritisation* (2016).

101 Gerhard Werle, *Africa and the International Criminal Court* (9789462650299 9462650292, T.M.C. Asser Press 2014); Kamari Maxine Clarke, *Africa and the ICC, perceptions of justice* (9781316556252, Cambridge University Press 2016).

102 See ICC-01/12-01/15.

precisely at circumventing the lack of state support for prosecuting the form of crime they are invested in. In contrast, the war on drugs and terrorism secured a narrative for the units that work on these crimes that almost effortlessly mobilises (essentially Weberian) ideas of state security.[103] While these narratives are not always explicit, they have been institutionalised through powerful national units specialising in these crimes and able to access the resources of the state. However, being placed close to state power does not entail that crime-fighting units have a similar role in the national bureaucracy, and despite their overlaps the war on drugs and the war on terror has been driven by different sections within domestic criminal justice systems. While drug units deal with this crime, often coordinating it at a national level, national intelligence agencies are the main suppliers of state knowledge of and protection from terrorism.

The second axis runs from a high to a low degree of corporate interest, and is related essentially to the value of crime fighting initiatives as a part of the exchange of commodities and services on a wider market. Here social structure of the war on drugs and transnational initiatives related to it lays bare how big pharmaceutical companies have invested in initiatives to fight drug related crime and to create drug free communities. Similarly, counter-terrorism is deeply engrained in a global security industry that develops and sells surveillance, crowd control and other solutions to governments and large companies alike. On the other end of the scale, while some companies have invested in anti-corruption initiatives, practitioners working with this crime and with environmental crime are usually far removed from corporate interests, not represented in the organising committees or boards behind international conferences in these sectors. Instead these spaces were characterised by NGO and advocacy activities aimed at raising awareness for the crime in question, a problem of less importance for the institutionally embedded crimes of drug trafficking and terrorism. This advocacy was driven by a mix of scholarly, practical and diplomatic expertise invested towards a reformatted international legal space in which institutional support for anti-corruption and the prosecution of environmental crimes. One similar strategy in these spaces was the attempts to make corruption and ecocide an international crime enforceable by an international criminal court. Here, ecocide seems to have been, at least very recently, more successful, perhaps due to the close social proximity of some of the professionals working to promote this crime and those active in the field of international criminal justice.

---

103 Cotterrell.

The third axis is related to geographical (and to some extent geopolitical) investments into these crimes. Drug trafficking and terrorism were heavily dominated by Western powers and defined by their control with these areas. While the drug war was essentially exported from the US by the DEA to the rest of the world, modern terrorism was conceptualised according to schemes of thought developed in industrialised democracies, that formed the basis for interventions on foreign countries and how this crime was defined at a regional and domestic level. While the push to make ecocide an international crime is tied especially to a European context, it is also supported from the Global South, especially by Indian activist such as Ela Gandhi, granddaughter of Mahatma Gandhi and a former MP in South Africa, and prominent environmental activist Vandana Shiva. The space of anti-corruption had wider geographical representation and featured prosecutors and advocates from much of the Global South who used transnational networks as a safety measure to avoid domestic push back and as a way of exchanging experiences with other professionals in similar positions. The structure of global power relations formats the space in which the four spaces of transnational crime exists and the political, symbolic and material resources invested towards them.

Since the social gravity of the four spaces of transnational criminal justice makes it difficult to conceptualise them as a single field in the sociological sense of the word, here inspired by Bourdieu, a central question is how these spaces are related. One common driving force in these spaces is the engagement of law enforcement that also forms the site for overlaps between organised crime, terrorism, corruption and, in some countries, ecocide prosecutions. However, most activities remain tied to specialised units within national systems, the strength of these being related to their proximity to state power and embeddedness in a wider bureaucracy. In this bureaucracy, there are significant overlaps between specialised offices, that link specific 'ecologies'[104] of practices through their criminal law expertise. The crimes they investigate are often intermingled and at a professional level, as agents circulate between different offices, some of which serve as hubs for specific forms of transnational contacts. This is the case, for instance, when it comes to extradition, which in the US system runs through the Office for International Assistance in the Department of Justice (DoJ). In different jurisdictions, centralised offices function as the main centres for specific types of transnational contacts. However, while the criminal justice professionals in the policing drugs, terror, corruption and ecological crime share important characteristics, the social gravity of

104 Andrew Abbott, 'Linked Ecologies:States and Universities as Environments for Professions' (Oxford, UK Malden, USA) 23 Sociological Theory 245.

these spaces themselves are very different and tied together at specific loci. At least conceptualised as oriented towards crime they are neighbouring spaces of practice in which national criminal justice systems play a crucial role. On the other hand, the war on drugs could perhaps also be seen as an outgrowth of a wider space of corporate pharmaceutics, although it also builds heavily on criminal justice technologies that fence off legal trade and consumption of drugs. Using Bourdieu's concepts, the precise definition of the boundaries of such spaces would require careful empirical investigation that takes the historical development of these spaces as their starting point.

However, while distinct social structuration of the four spaces of transnational criminal justice does lay bare crucial differences that make it hard to conceptualise them as one field of practice, the four spaces are not necessarily fields in their own right. As the three also highlight, the four spaces are placed very differently in the domestic criminal justice system, terrorism and drug control being part of the core of policing and closely attuned to the policies of the state and anti-corruption and the fight against ecocide holding a less established position in national and international law enforcement. The different social and political positions of the practices aimed at curbing these crimes have within criminal justice systems as well as the distinct composition of their stakeholders, can be conceptualised by following the claims they make about the role of criminal justice. This can also give important clues about the field of practice to which the identified spaces of transnational criminal justice belong and that shape their practices. In the case of terrorism and drug enforcement, law enforcement is seen as a security mechanism that defends society against outside forces and thus is closely related to the right hand of the state. This is evident from the stakeholders as well as their position-taking on specific issues related to these crimes. These spaces frame their practices as security and could be said to position themselves in a larger transnational field of security.[105] On the other hand, the practices that dominate the spaces of anti-corruption and ending of ecocide often target the practices of the state or that of large companies. As such, they are less focused on bringing security, although both spaces at times frame and legitimate their practices towards this end, than they are on creating good and sustainable governance. As such, these spaces are related to what can be conceptualised as a larger field of transnational governance and use criminal justice as a tool in this regard.

Here a return to the legal frameworks provides one clue to understanding the constitution of such fields. The identified fields do overlap not only

105 Bigo, 'Delivering Liberty and Security? The Reframing of Freedom when Associated with Security'.

practically, but build on similar forms of legislation and transnational criminalisation, the UN Convention against Transnational Organised Crime (UNTOC), for instance, cutting across spaces. In terms of the social constitution of these fields, one based on security and one on governance, there are also significant overlaps. At the national and transnational level, security and governance are related although they typically mobilise different state resources. This is also visible in the criminal justice professionals working with the four crimes. While specialised national units dealing with different crimes and the transnational networks may compete internally, some of the agents engaged with different crimes are repeat players that shift attention from one crime to the next depending on which is in political vogue and undergoing development. This demonstrates both the professional value ascribed to specific practices, professionals moving to spaces where there is more prestige, typically for law enforcement closer to the pole of security, and how political priorities change, terrorism, for instance, moving up the political agenda since the turn of the millennium. In response to changing political priorities and in an effort to influence them, all of the identified spaces build on criminal law technologies, or at least have stakeholders who aspire to do so, and enter some of the same political arenas where they essentially compete for attention and resources. This is clear particularly in the efforts to promote drug trafficking, terrorism, corruption and environmental crime as the next international crime, but is also visible in domestic 'palace battles' between ministries, law enforcement agencies and other stakeholders. The four identified spaces are linked through their reliance on criminal justice technologies and imaginaries, but also operate through distinct range of other interests, embodied in career trajectories characterised by investments in specific transnational issues either by NGO advocates or corporate professionals. It is the balance between these stakeholders that structures the identified fields in which criminal law is but one, if centrally placed, tool aimed at creating either higher degrees of security or good governance.

Concluding Remarks

In sociological terms, transnational criminal justice is difficult to conceptualise as a unified field of practice. It is more intelligible as a cluster of separate spaces that share some social and political dynamics that are precisely related to the crafting and development of new forms of criminal justice beyond the state. These initiatives exist in a wider space characterised by what could be called the fields of transnational security and governance, where criminal law technologies and ideals compete with other perspectives on how best to deal with specific problems. These fields are also characterised by the contest to prioritise resources and classify usages of the law, something that is evident for instance in the division of the space of anti-corruption between criminal law and compliance professionals. In this wider global environment, the promotion of criminal law initiatives binds the four analysed spaces together. The idea of a 'system' of TCL cuts across these spaces of practice to conceptualise the larger legal framework that has emerged since the fall of the Cold War. To understand the linkages between what can be conceived in legal terms as a coherent system, and what in a sociological sense appears to be distinct, yet interconnected spaces of practice characterised by their proximity to either security or good governance, an increased scholarly dialogue between the two disciplines generate new knowledge about how social fields affect legal developments and how new legal instruments affect the social and professional balances of such fields.

However, significant questions still go unanswered in relation to how these separate spaces or fields interpret and use the rules of which TCL exists. If this system of law indeed creates '"fictional transnational legal space", as pointed out by Neil Boister in this volume and if this legal space is driven by stakeholders as different from the ones identified in this article, social scientists and legal scholars alike face the challenge of explaining precisely why law enforcement agencies, policy advocates and business interests use specific legal instruments among the many that compose TCL and how they interpret these frameworks. Precisely how separate social spaces and fields are related and what shapes the gravity of the wider cluster of which they are part, is highly complex and must be studied empirically. Investigating how the social intricacies of specific fields of practice are bound to legal intricacies (understood here as how the law is perceived, used and developed) would potentially lay bare what binds the four spaces identified in this article together as constellations in a larger field of transnational security and governance, and how the relations between these fields shape their development.

www.ingramcontent.com/pod-product-compliance
Lightning Source LLC
Chambersburg PA
CBHW031328230926
51848CB00001B/142